The Icarus Deception

Art is frightening.

Art isn't pretty.

Art isn't painting.

Art isn't something you hang on the wall.

Art is what we do when we're truly alive.

If you've already decided that you're not an artist, it's worth considering why you made that decision and what it might take to unmake it.

If you've announced that you have no talent (in anything!), then you're hiding.

Art might scare you.

Art might bust you.

But art is who we are and what we do and what we need.

An artist is someone who uses bravery, insight, creativity and boldness to challenge the status quo. And an artist takes it (all of it: the work, the process, the feedback from those we seek to connect with) personally.

Art isn't a result; it's a journey. The challenge of our time is to find a journey worthy of your heart and your soul.

ABOUT THE AUTHOR

Seth Godin is the author of fourteen international bestsellers, including *Purple Cow, The Dip, Tribes, Linchpin* and *Poke the Box*. He is also the founder and CEO of Squidoo.com and one of the most popular business bloggers in the world.

Visit www.SethGodin.com and click on his head.

The
ICARUS
DECEPTION

How High Will You Fly?

SETH GODIN

PORTFOLIO
PENGUIN

PORTFOLIO PENGUIN

Published by the Penguin Group
Penguin Books Ltd, 80 Strand, London WC2R 0RL, England
Penguin Group (USA) Inc., 375 Hudson Street, New York, New York 10014, USA
Penguin Group (Canada), 90 Eglinton Avenue East, Suite 700, Toronto, Ontario, Canada M4P 2Y3
(a division of Pearson Penguin Canada Inc.)
Penguin Ireland, 25 St Stephen's Green, Dublin 2, Ireland (a division of Penguin Books Ltd)
Penguin Group (Australia), 707 Collins Street, Melbourne, Victoria 3008, Australia
(a division of Pearson Australia Group Pty Ltd)
Penguin Books India Pvt Ltd, 11 Community Centre, Panchsheel Park, New Delhi – 110 017, India
Penguin Group (NZ), 67 Apollo Drive, Rosedale, Auckland 0632, New Zealand
(a division of Pearson New Zealand Ltd)
Penguin Books (South Africa) (Pty) Ltd, Block D, Rosebank Office Park,
181 Jan Smuts Avenue, Parktown North, Gauteng 2193, South Africa

Penguin Books Ltd, Registered Offices: 80 Strand, London WC2R 0RL, England

www.penguin.com

First published in the United States of America by Portfolio/Penguin,
a member of Penguin Group (USA) Inc. 2012
First published in Great Britain by Portfolio Penguin 2012
007

Copyright © Do You Zoom, Inc., 2012

The moral right of the author has been asserted

Excerpt from 'when god decided to invent' from *Complete Poems: 1904–1962*
by E. E. Cummings, edited by George J. Firmage.
Copyright 1944, © 1972, 1991 by the Trustees for the E. E. Cummings Trust.
Used by permission of Liveright Publishing Corporation.

'Le Saut dans le vide' ('Leap into the Void') by Yves Klein. © Yves Klein, ADAGP, Paris (for the work).
Photo: Harry Shunk-John Kender. Shunk-Kender © Roy Lichtenstein Foundation.

Printed in Great Britain by Clays Ltd, Elcograf S.p.A.

A CIP catalogue record for this book is available from the British Library

ISBN: 978–0–670–92292–5

www.greenpenguin.co.uk

Dedicated to Tom Peters, Hugh MacLeod, Walter Dean Myers, Dan Pink, Sarah Kay, Kevin Kelly, Cory Doctorow, Susan Piver, Steven Pressfield, Pema Chödron, Zig Ziglar, Jay Levinson, Amanda Palmer, Neil Gaiman, Brené Brown, and all the fellow travelers who cared enough to stand up and say, "here."

We Are All Artists Now

How Long Are You Going to Wait?

They told you to get your résumé in order, to punch your ticket, to fit in, and to follow instructions.

They told you to swallow your pride, not to follow your dream.

They promised trinkets and prizes and possibly riches if you would just suck it up and be part of the system, if you would merely do what you were told and conform.

They sold you debt and self-storage and reality TV shows. They sold your daughters and sons, too.

All in exchange for what would happen later, when it was your turn.

It's your turn.

You Are Not Your Career

Your ability to follow instructions is not the secret to your success.

You are hiding your best work, your best insight, and your best self from us every day.

We know how much you care, and it's a shame that the system

works overtime to push you away from the people and the projects you care about.

The world does not owe you a living, but just when you needed it, a door was opened for you to make a difference.

It's too bad that so much time has been wasted, but it would be unforgivable to wait any longer. You have the ability to contribute so much. We need you, now.

"Does Anyone Have Any Suggestions?"

We've all heard this request at the end of a meeting. Sometimes the moderator even means it. Sometimes the moderator, the boss, the person with a problem, actually wants to know if the group has an untried concept or an insight to share.

And the response is always the same. Silence. Sidelong glances, perhaps some shuffling of papers, but still, silence.

Really?

All these highly trained, well-paid, and respected people in a room and not one person has something to contribute? I doubt it.

Stick around for a few minutes, and if the moderator has earned any trust at all, someone speaks up. And if that person isn't summarily executed, someone else speaks up. And then more people. Until finally, the room is filled with energy, a buzz that you can feel. Finally, we're permitted to be human, to end the silence, to share our best work.

Amazingly, everyone in the room is capable of seeing and analyzing and solving. Everyone in the room is capable of passion. Everyone in the room can care enough to do something—if they can overthrow the self-induced, systemically amplified censor that keeps them in line.

Why didn't anyone speak up earlier? Why did we have to wait until the meeting was over? Where does the strained silence come from?

This isn't a book for other people. This is a book for you. It's a book for anyone who has been overlooked or brainwashed or seduced into being invisible.

A revolution is here, our revolution, and it is shining a light on what we've known deep down for a long time—you are capable of making a difference, of being bold, and of changing more than you are willing to admit. You are capable of making art.

Green Eggs and Ham

This might not work.

This book might not hit its mark, or it might not be direct enough (or it might be too direct). I've gone outside my comfort zone in writing and publishing it, and I'm hoping you'll go out of your comfort zone in reading it.

I'm trying to help you see something that's all around but that you may have missed, something you may be intentionally ignoring. I'm working to get more people to taste something they haven't wanted to taste, to experience a different way of working and thinking about the work they do.

It's so tempting for me to smooth out the edges, to make this work safe and obvious and comforting. I wish I could make the book easy and guaranteed and reach everyone I want to reach. I can't do that, though.

This revolution is too important to allow me to water down this project. Thank you for letting me take the risk of writing this book, and thank you for taking the risk of giving it a try.

Catching the Wily Fox

Build an eight-foot-long wooden fence in the forest.

Lay out some bait and then go away for a week.

The fox is too crafty to be caught in a simple trap, and he will smell you and avoid the fence for days. But eventually, he'll come and eat the bait.

At the end of the week, build a second length of fence at a right angle to the first. Leave more bait.

The fox will avoid the fence again for a few days, then take the bait.

At the end of the second week, build a third wall and a gate. Leave more bait.

When you come back at the end of a month, the fox will be happily prancing in his safe enclosure, and all you will have to do is close the gate. The fox will be trapped.

This, of course, is what happened to us. The industrial age built the trap we're mired in, but it didn't build the trap all at once; that took centuries to perfect. And we were seduced. Seduced by the bait of decent pay and plenty of prizes. Seduced by the apparent security of the enclosure. And once the gate was shut, we were kept in by the threat of shame, the amplification of risk, and society's reliance on more and shinier prizes.

For us, though, the situation is even more poignant than it is for the fox. As the industrial age has faded away and been replaced by the connection economy—the wide-open reality of our new economic revolution—the fence has been dismantled. It's gone.

But most of us have no idea that we're no longer fenced in. We've been so thoroughly brainwashed and intimidated and socialized that we stay huddled together, waiting for instructions, when we have the first, best, and once-in-a-lifetime chance to do something extraordinary instead.

This book revolves around a simple assumption on my part: that you know how to be human and how to make art. We don't need to be taught to make art, but sometimes we need permission to do so. Following instructions is overrated.

CONTENTS

PART THREE
Grit and Art and the Work That's Worth Doing

The path available to us is to gum up the works, stand firm, and pick ourselves.

PART FOUR
Shame, Vulnerability, and Being Naked

Of course it's difficult and frightening. When we do art, we put ourselves at risk, because risk is part of what makes it art.

PART FIVE
To Make Art, Think Like an Artist. To Connect, Be Human.

More than eighty-seven ideas to chew on.

APPENDIX ONE
True-Life Stories of Fourteen Real Artists

Could be you.

APPENDIX TWO
V Is for Vulnerable: An Artist's Abecedary

An alphabet for artists.

ACKNOWLEDGMENTS

PART ZERO

Art, the Comfort Zone, and the Chance of a Lifetime

Why Make Art?

Because you must. The new connected economy demands it and will reward you for nothing else.

Because you can. Art is what it is to be human.

The Icarus Deception

Just south of the Greek island of Samos lies the Icarian Sea. Legend has it that this is where Icarus died—a victim of his hubris.

His father, Daedalus, was a master craftsman. Banished to prison for sabotaging the work of King Minos (captor of the Minotaur), Daedalus created a brilliant escape plot, described in the myth that we were told as children.

He fashioned a set of wings for himself and his son. After affixing the wings with wax, they set out to escape. Daedalus warned Icarus not to fly too close to the sun. Entranced by his magical ability to fly, Icarus disobeyed and flew too high. We all know what happened next: The wax melted, and Icarus, the beloved son, lost his wings, tumbled into the sea, and died.

The lesson of this myth: Don't disobey the king. Don't disobey your dad. Don't imagine that you're better than you are, and most of all, don't ever believe that you have the ability to do what a god might do.

The part of the myth you weren't told: In addition to telling Icarus not to fly too high, Daedalus instructed his son not to fly too low, too close to the sea, because the water would ruin the lift in his wings.

Society has altered the myth, encouraging us to forget the part about the sea, and created a culture where we constantly remind one another about the dangers of standing up, standing out, and making a ruckus. Industrialists have made hubris a cardinal sin but conveniently ignored a far more common failing: settling for too little.

It's far more dangerous to fly too low than too high, because it feels *safe* to fly low. We settle for low expectations and small dreams and guarantee ourselves less than we are capable of. By flying too low, we shortchange not only ourselves but also those who depend on us or might benefit from our work. We're so obsessed about the risk of shining brightly that we've traded in everything that matters to avoid it.

The path that's available to each of us is neither reckless stupidity nor mindless compliance. No, the path that's available to us is to be human, to do art, and to fly far higher than we've been taught is possible. We've built a world where it's possible to fly higher than ever, and the tragedy is that we've been seduced into believing that we ought to fly ever lower instead.

Your Comfort Zone (Versus Your Safety Zone)

For a long time, the two were one and the same. The mountain climber who knows when she's outside of her safety zone feels uncomfortable about it and stops—and lives to climb another day.

Your entire life has been about coordinating your comfort zone and your safety zone. Learning when to push and when to back off, understanding how it feels when you're about to hit a danger zone. Like the fox, we've been trained to stay inside the fence, because inside the fence is where it's safe—until it's too late.

We don't have time to reevaluate the safety zone every time we make a decision, so over time, we begin to forget about the safety zone and merely pay attention to its twin sister, the comfort zone. We assume that what makes us comfortable also makes us safe.

The fence holding us back is no longer there, but we still feel comfortable with the old boundaries. Now that a revolution has hit, now that the economy is upside down and the rules have changed, we have to confront an obvious truth:

The safety zone has changed, but your comfort zone has not. Those places that felt safe—the corner office, the famous college, the secure job—aren't. You're holding back, betting on a return to normal, but in the new normal, your resistance to change is no longer helpful.

We made a mistake. We settled for a safety zone that wasn't bold enough, that embraced authority and compliance. We built our comfort zone around being obedient and invisible, and as a result, we're far too close to the waves.

You can go to as many meetings as you want, read as many books, and attend as many seminars as you like, but if you don't figure out how to realign your comfort zone with today's new safety zone, all the strategy in the world isn't going to help you.

It's simple. There's still a safety zone, but it's not in a place that feels comfortable to you. The new safety zone is the place where art and innovation and destruction and rebirth happen. The new safety zone is the never-ending creation of ever-deeper personal connection.

Moving to a new safety zone is a little like learning to swim. It's clearly better to have the ability to survive (and even have fun) in the water, but for a long time it's not comfortable. Recognizing that the safety zone has moved might be the prompt you need to re-evaluate your comfort zone.

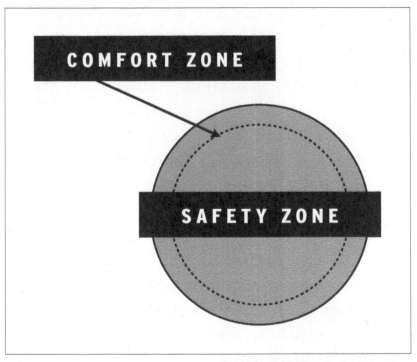

Successful people align their comfort zone with the behavior that keeps them safe.

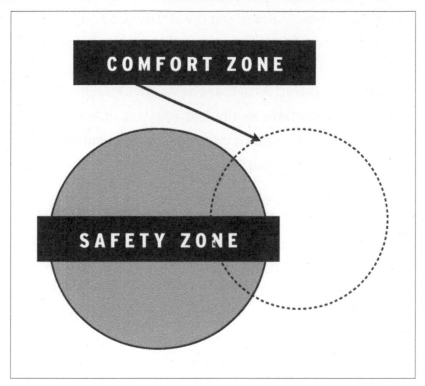

But what happens when the place of safety moves . . . and you don't?

If you become someone who is uncomfortable unless she is creating change, restless if things are standing still, and disappointed if you haven't failed recently, you've figured out how to become comfortable with the behaviors most likely to make you safe going forward.

Art Is the New Safety Zone

Creating ideas that spread and connecting the disconnected are the two pillars of our new society, and both of them require the posture of the artist.

Doing these two things regularly and with abandon is where the new safety zone lies. Maintaining the status quo and fighting to fit in no longer work, because our economy and our culture have changed.

The bad news is this: Artists are never invulnerable. This safety zone isn't as comfortable as the last one was. It took a hundred years for us to be brainwashed into accepting the industrial system as normal and safe. It is neither, not for long.

Forget Salvador Dalí

When you hear the word "artist," do you picture the slightly crazed Dalí or the self-destructive Jackson Pollock? Perhaps you've been trained to imagine that you need to be someone like Johnny Depp or Amanda F. Palmer in order to make art.

This notion is both dangerous and wrong.

Oscar Wilde wrote that art is "new, complex, and vital." Art isn't something that's made by artists. *Artists are people who make art.*

Art is not a gene or a specific talent. Art is an attitude, culturally driven and available to anyone who chooses to adopt it. Art isn't something sold in a gallery or performed on a stage. Art is the unique work of a human being, work that touches another. Most painters, it turns out, aren't artists at all—they are safety-seeking copycats.

Seizing new ground, making connections between people or ideas, working without a map—these are works of art, and if you do them, you are an artist, regardless of whether you wear a smock, use a computer, or work with others all day long.

Speaking up when there's no obvious right answer, making yourself vulnerable when it's possible to put up shields, and caring about both the process and the outcome—these are works of art that our society embraces and the economy demands.

Tactics Are No Replacement for Art

Understanding cutting-edge business concepts like the Long Tail and the Tipping Point and Purple Cow and GTD and the rest is worthless if you don't commit. Commit to the frightening work of flying blind, of taking a stand, and of making something new, complex, and vital—or nothing much happens.

These cutting-edge strategies and tactics seem to promise a pain-free way to achieve your goals. You can read about a new strategy, find a guaranteed, impersonal way to achieve, point the industrial machine at a new market niche or a new sort of note-taking technique or buzzword and, presto, results without pain. Ideaviruses will be unleashed, points will be tipped, and tails will get longer.

Alas, there isn't a pain-free way to achieve your goals.

I've read these books. I've written some of them. And I love them all, but the ideas are not enough without commitment. They're not enough because strategy is empty without change, empty without passion, and empty without people willing to confront the void.

I've seen the frightened looks in the eyes of an audience of music industry execs as they contemplate the death of their industry (and the possibilities that lie in its rebirth). I've heard the ennui in the voice of yet another manager at yet another endless meeting. And I've witnessed countless opportunities squandered by people who could have taken action but didn't. Not because they couldn't figure out what to do but because they weren't willing to do it.

Microsoft and Sony Records and the local freelancer have all squandered clear and obvious opportunities—not through ignorance of what was on offer but because it was easier to avoid committing to a new way of thinking.

Strategy and tactics live on the outside, in the cold world of consultants and spreadsheets. They are things we do without changing the way we think. Art, on the other hand, is personal, built on attitude and vision and commitment.

This is a book about committing to do work that is personal, that requires guts, and that has the potential to change everything. Art is the act of a human being doing generous work, creating something for the first time, touching another person.

This is a book about why each of us should make art. Why it's worth the price. And why we can't wait.

The world is filled with ordinary people doing extraordinary things.

Art Is Frightening

Art isn't pretty.

Art isn't painting.

Art isn't something you hang on the wall.

Art is what we do when we're truly alive.

If you've already decided that you're not an artist, it's worth considering why you made that decision and what it might take to unmake it.

If you've announced that you have no talent (in anything!), then you're hiding.

Art might scare you.

Art might bust you.

But art is who we are and what we do and what we need.

An artist is someone who uses bravery, insight, creativity, and boldness to challenge the status quo. And an artist takes it (all of it, the work, the process, the feedback from those we seek to connect with) personally.

Art isn't a result; it's a journey. The challenge of our time is to find a journey worthy of your heart and your soul.

Not an Artist?

That's the easy answer. Artists are other people. They don't dress or act or do work like we do. They're not required to go to meetings, they're full of themselves, they have tattoos, and they have talent.

But of course, this is nonsense.

When you were rewarded for obedience, you were obedient.

When you were rewarded for compliance, you were compliant.

When you were rewarded for competence, you were competent.

Now that society finally values art, it's time to make art.

Quality Is Assumed

We assume that you will make something to spec.

We assume that the lights will go on when we flip the switch.

We assume that the answer is in Wikipedia.

All we're willing to pay you extra for is what we don't assume, what we can't get easily and regularly and for free. We need you to provide the things that are unexpected, scarce, and valuable.

Scarcity and abundance have been flipped. High-quality work

is no longer scarce. Competence is no longer scarce, either. We have too many good choices—there's an abundance of things to buy and people to hire.

What's scarce is trust, connection, and surprise. These are three elements in the work of a successful artist.

The New Scarcity

One kind of scarcity involves effort. You can put in only so many hours, sweat only so much. The employer pays for effort, because he can't get effort he can count on for free. And the eager-beaver employee expends extra effort to make a mark but soon learns that it doesn't scale.

Another kind of scarcity involves physical resources. Resources keep getting more scarce, because we're running out of them. Paradoxically, we're also running out of places in our houses to store our junk and running out of room in our bodies to store what we eat.

The new, third kind of scarcity is the emotional labor of art. The risk involved in digging deep to connect and surprise, the patience required to build trust, the guts necessary to say, "I made this"— these are all scarce and valuable. And they scale.

Here Come the Noisemakers

You are chaos, and there is nothing to keep you out.

When network engineers think about the security of the network, they begin with a firewall. The firewall is designed to keep unwanted information and viruses out of the system.

The Internet doesn't have a firewall. We're all able to connect.

We each represent the ghost in the machine, the noise, the one who might change everything.

What you feed the network changes what you get back. The network connects people to one another, people to organizations, and best of all, people to ideas.

This new network celebrates art, enables connections, helps tribes to form, amplifies weirdness, and spreads ideas. What it cannot abide is boredom.

If you want to write, here's a blog. Write. Today, writers like Xeni Jardin and Danielle LaPorte reach millions without the blessing of big media.

If you want to sing or make videos, well, sure, YouTube will happily show your work to the masses. Judson Laipply has already entertained more than a hundred million people with his short film—a video that cost exactly zero to film.

If you want to share an invention or fund a project or topple a government, the connected economy makes it easier to do that than ever before.

Can you imagine it getting *less* open? This is just the beginning.

Revolutions bring total chaos. That's what makes them revolutionary.

A Nonhierarchy of Artists

The painter in front of a blank canvas. The architect changing the rules of construction. The playwright who makes us cry. The doctor who cares enough to call. The detective who cracks a cold case. The diva with a new interpretation of a classic. The customer service rep who, despite the distance and the rush, makes an honest connection. The entrepreneur who dares to start without permission or authority. The middle manager who transforms the key meeting with a single comment.

You?

The Evolution of "Fine Art"

James Elkins points out that schools of art used to divide the arts into only two categories: fine art and industrial art.

Then the intellectuals expanded the categories to: painting, sculpture, architecture, music, and poetry.

From there it's a quick leap to: performance, video, film, photography, fiber, weaving, silkscreen, ceramics, interior architecture, industrial design, fashion, artists' books, printmaking, kinetic sculpture, computing, neon, and holography.

To which I'd add: entrepreneurship, customer service, invention, technology, connection, leadership, and a dozen others. These are the new performing arts, the valuable visual arts, the essential personal arts.

Welcome to the Connection Economy

The value we create is directly related to how much valuable information we can produce, how much trust we can earn, and how often we innovate.

In the industrial economy, the stuff we made (literally stuff—widgets, devices, and O-rings) comprised the best assets we could build. Fortunes belonged to men who built railroads, lightbulbs, and buildings. Today we're seeking something a revolution apart from that sort of productivity.

The connection economy rewards the leader, the initiator, and the rebel.

The Internet wasn't built to make it easy for you to watch Lady Gaga videos. The Internet is a connection machine, and anyone with a laptop or a smartphone is now connected to just about everyone else. And it turns out that those connections are changing the world.

If your factory burns down but you have loyal customers, you'll be fine. On the other hand, if you lose your customers, even your factory isn't going to help you—Detroit is filled with empty factories.

If your team is filled with people who work for the company, you'll soon be defeated by tribes of people who work for a cause.

If you use your money to buy advertising to promote the average products you produce for average people, soon you'll run out of money. But if you use your money to make exceptional products and services, you won't need to spend it on advertising, because your customers will connect to one another and bring you more.

The connection economy has changed how you get a job and what you do when you get to that job. It has changed how we make and listen to music, write and read books, and discover where to eat, what to eat, and whom to eat with. It has destroyed the mediocre middle of average products for average people who have few choices, and it has enabled the weird edges, where people who care find others who care and they all end up caring about something even more than they did before they met.

The connection economy enables endless choice and endless

shelf space and puts a premium on attention and on trust, neither of which is endless.

Most of all, the connection economy has made competence not particularly valuable and has replaced it with an insatiable desire for things that are new, real, and important.

New, Real, and Important

Those are three elements that define art.

The connection economy functions on a steady diet of new, real, and important. The connection economy builds a new asset, one that we can measure and value now for the first time. Suddenly, it's not the building or the rules or the packaging that matters; it's the bridges between people that generate value, and those bridges are built by art.

Art is difficult, risky, and frightening.
It's also the only option if we choose to care.

The Opposite of Coherent . . .

It's not incoherent.

There's only one way to organize a deck of cards in order. There's just one way to stack the dishes according to the manual. The industrial economy embraces coherence.

Art, on the other hand, is almost never coherent. It's messy and comes in fits and starts. It's difficult to write a table of contents or outline for. It's unpredictable.

And it demands our attention. It works the way our brains do, not the way our machines do.

It's impossible to talk coherently about art. That doesn't mean you can't understand it.

The opposite of coherent is interesting.

Changing Your Framework for Success

Competent people enjoy being competent. Once you're good at something, changing what you do or moving to a new way of doing it will be stressful because it will make you (momentarily) incompetent.

Art is threatening because it always involves moving away from the comfort zone into the unknown. The unknown is the black void, the place where failure can happen (and so can success). Our instinct, then, particularly if we're successful at one thing, is to avoid the unknown. To stay in the comfort zone and ignore the fact that the safety zone has moved.

No one taught you how to do art. There are generations of thinking about what it means to challenge your fear and create something worth talking about—something that changes people— so you don't have to start from scratch. If you decide that it's important to stop complying and start creating, the first thing to do is change your framework, the worldview you bring to your work.

The framework changes what we see and changes what we tell ourselves is important. And the revolution is tearing your old framework down.

The Chance of a Lifetime

No one enjoys watching their house burn down. Revolutions do that. They destroy the perfect, disrupt the status quo, and change everything.

And then they enable the impossible.

The chance that each of us has is clear: The connection revolution is shuffling the deck and enabling new organizations and new ideas to thrive. Someone is going to be leading us; someone is going to be exploring the edges; someone is going to be creating things of incalculable value.

What happened yesterday is over. Tomorrow the door is wide open, and this is your chance to connect.

I Categorically Reject Your Cynicism

Art is not for "other people."

All of those people who you say are your artistic heroes . . . All of those people who have made such a difference in the world . . . None of those people were ordained. None of those people were preapproved. None of those people were considered all-stars at an early age.

So please, please don't tell me you have to be a born artist to do art. I'm not buying it.

Your Pain Is Real

It's the pain of possibility, vulnerability, and risk. Once you stop feeling it, you've lost your best chance to make a difference.

The easiest way to avoid the pain is to lull it to sleep by finding a job that numbs you. Soon the pain of the artist will be replaced by a different sort of pain, the pain of the cog, the pain of someone who knows that his gifts are being wasted and that his future is out of his control.

It's not a worthwhile trade. In the words of Joseph Campbell, you're doing art "for the experience of being alive." The alternative is to be numb, to lull yourself into the false sense of security offered by the promise of the rare well-paid job where you are doing someone else's bidding.

The pain is part of being alive. Art is the narrative of being alive.

Like a growth spurt for a teenager, the pain of facing the void where art lives is part of the deal, our stretching into a better self.

Redefining Courage

Courage doesn't always involve physical heroism in the face of death. It doesn't always require giant leaps worthy of celebration. Sometimes, courage is the willingness to speak the truth about what you see and to own what you say.

In order for there to be courage, of course, there must be risk. It doesn't take courage to open the refrigerator, because there's no downside. No, courage is necessary because owning our point of view brings risk. When you speak your truth, you have opened a door, allowing others to speak to you, directly to you, to your true self.

Courage is telling our story,
not being immune to criticism.

—Brené Brown

If It Doesn't Ship, It's Not Art

Art always involves a collision with a marketplace, an interaction with a recipient, a gift given and a gift received.

You can plan and sketch and curse the system all day, but if you don't ship, you haven't done your work, because the work involves *connection* and the generosity behind it. It's entirely possible that one day your insight will be discovered and that it will touch someone or make a difference. But if you hide your contribution from us, you can't be considered an artist, because it's not art until a human connection is made.

We're not waiting for you to tell us about your notebook filled with ideas. Tell us about the connections you have enabled and the impact you have made instead.

What Do You Make?

Make connections.

Make a difference.

Make a ruckus.

Make a legacy.

The economy has rescinded the simple offer of "Do what you're told, play it safe, and you can make a living." Making a living is now harder than ever. The alternatives are up to you.

We've been trained to prefer being right to learning something, to prefer passing the test to making a difference, and most of all, to prefer fitting in with the right people, the people with economic power. Now it's your turn to stand up and stand out.

Most People Don't Believe They Are Capable of Initiative

Initiating a project, a blog, a Wikipedia article, even a unique family journey. Initiating something particularly when you're not putatively in charge. We avoid these acts because we've been trained to avoid them.

At the same time, almost all people believe they are capable of editing, giving feedback, or merely criticizing.

That means that finding people to fix your typos is easy. Finding someone to say "go" is almost impossible.

I don't think the shortage of artists has much to do with the innate ability to create or initiate. I think it has to do with believing that it's possible and acceptable for you to do it. We've had these doors open wide for only a decade or so, and most people have been brainwashed into believing that their job is to copyedit the world, not to design it.

Quick Question Before We Go On . . .

Do you think we don't need your art, or are you afraid to produce it?

PART ONE

The Connection Economy Demands That We Create Art

Opportunities Amid the Junk

Just outside Harvard Square, at 29 Oxford Street, lies the Cruft Lab. Part of the physics department at Harvard, this is where George Washington Pierce invented the crystal oscillator about a hundred years ago. Without his invention, radio stations would never have been commercially feasible.

But Cruft Hall is even more important for giving its name to a vitally important concept. "Cruft" is the engineering term for the leftover detritus, useless computer code, broken devices, empty boxes, and junk that we have to maneuver around as technology advances.

Over the decades, abandoned radar components, obsolete circuit boards, and outdated vacuum tubes began to pile up in the lab. The windows were stacked full of cruft, things that used to be important but were now simply in the way.

Revolutions eliminate the perfect and enable the impossible. They also overwhelm us with cruft.

The art of moving forward lies in understanding what to leave behind.

The simplest plan is to keep it all, to embrace what worked before, and to hide, mostly to hide, from the open vistas of the new postrevolutionary world. It's so easy to do, and if the world moves slowly enough, you can even do it successfully for a while.

No longer. The industrial age, the one that established our schooling, our workday, our economy, and our expectations, is dying. It's dying faster than most of us expected, and it's causing plenty of pain, indecision, and fear as it goes.

We're surrounded by the cruft of the industrial age, by the expectations, beliefs, and standards of an era that's now over.

What an opportunity. To be among the first to clean it out, to ignore it, to move to a different building altogether. A life without cruft slowing you down, a career with a focus on what you can create instead of what you must replicate.

The Achieving Society

In 1959, psychologist and sociologist David McClelland published a breakthrough treatise on why some moments in history are filled with rapid growth while others are not. He studied why some cultures miss out on advancement while others succeed.

It turns out that it's not race or climate or even the power of charismatic leadership that leads to boom times. The Renaissance, Silicon Valley, or the explosion of culture in France in the late 1800s are all cultural and technical breakthroughs that we'd like to repeat. While technology might be a contributing factor, more than anything else, achievement comes from a culture that celebrates the achievement motive.

In countries and regions and moments of time when there is a cultural imperative to make art and to move forward, things change for the better. It seems obvious as I write this, but the correlated element of success always seems to be that there are many individuals who *care enough to want to succeed.*

Using a series of clever tests, McClelland and his colleagues tested thousands of subjects, asking them to describe their daydreams and to tell stories about what they hoped to do in the future. What they found was that the *n* achievement score (a simple count of how often these stories indicated a need for achievement) gave extraordinary insight into a host of decisions that people made in their work lives.

A high *n* achievement score, for example, meant that you were far more likely to have "better memory," be "more apt to volunteer as subjects for psychological experiments," and even be "more resistant to social pressure." It also meant that you'd do better at scrambled word puzzles.

The question, as we move from an industrial economy that cherishes compliance to a connected economy that prizes achievement, is this: Are we supporting this shift with a culture that encourages us to dream important dreams? What do we challenge our achievers to do? When do we encourage or demand that they move from standardized tests and Dummies guides to work that actually matters?

More Than Your Parents Made

If I were giving a high school graduation speech in 1920, here's what I'd say:

Congratulations, men! You have made it through school, and now it's time to go to work. Go get a job at General Electric in Schenectady. Sign up to do whatever work the boss tells you to do. Work on the line that makes lightbulbs, or work on the line that makes transformers. Stick with it; keep your head down and your nose to the grindstone.

It's a good job, steady work, and fair pay. In 1960, forty years from now, you will retire, with an excellent pension and a small house that's paid for. You will make more money than your parents ever did eking out a living growing corn.

Then, if I were invited back fifteen or twenty years later, to talk to their kids at their graduation, I might say:

Boys and girls, the future is here, and it's called college. Your parents worked hard to get you this far, but you're not done yet. Go to college and broaden your mind, learn to manage, to organize, to become a middle manager.

Four years from now, perhaps you can get a job managing workers at any of the Generals—General Dynamics or General Motors or, yes, General Electric. The Generals need you to help them organize their burgeoning workforces.

It's steady work and it pays well, too.

A few years after that, my advice would probably push them into one of the professions. The next step up the ladder is to become a doctor or a lawyer.

And when the mass-marketing age of television was upon us, we would encourage the next generation to become marketers, advertisers, copywriters, and investment bankers—workers who manipulate ideas, not iron. The work is totally abstract compared with the work of these kids' grandparents, but once again, it's a notch up the ladder.

Which brings us to today. What's the next step? Farmer to worker to manager to professional to commercial intellectual to . . .

First-World Problems (First-World Opportunities)

The nuts in first class aren't warm. Instagram wasn't available on Android for months. I had to wait more than a minute for a tech-support operator. None of this is fair. And now the greatest indignity: Who moved my safety zone?

It's easy to become a self-parody, whining about the imperfections in an almost perfect world that gets more perfect all the time. We finally got the industrial world working the way it was supposed to; we found our safe spot, our mortgage and our house and our dream in the suburbs.

The connection revolution has made it easier to find what we want, get what we want, and complain about what we didn't get.

But it has also opened a door that has never been opened before.

With all the polished perfection of the privileged world we live in, we've also been given a huge opportunity. The network has offered to connect us to one another, and those connections are as valuable as any widget.

The value of information became obvious when *TV Guide* (the magazine with information about when certain shows were on) sold for more money than the networks themselves were worth. Information about the content was worth more than the content.

And now companies realize that the time their employees spend with customers (and the loyalty and enthusiasm it generates) creates more value than does the machine in the factory that cuts out pieces of steel.

Again and again, our success turns not on being the low-price leader but on being the high-trust leader.

The challenge of our future isn't to ensure that the seat warmer in our sixty-thousand-dollar sedan is functioning properly; the challenge is to take advantage of this brief moment in time, a time when connection is easier to find and cherish than it will ever be again. While some people are polishing their systems and honing their spreadsheets, an ever-growing cadre of artists is busy creating work that's worth connecting to.

The connection economy, while it enables miracles every day, also destroys the value in what used to be our safety zone.

Don't worry about your stuff. Worry about making meaning instead.

First, Capitalism Enabled Workers to Create Value . . .

The butcher and the baker make a trade. The butcher gets a loaf of bread in exchange for a piece of meat, and both benefit. The bread is made far more efficiently by the baker than the butcher could ever create it.

Soon the baker had made enough trades that he could buy a better oven. Now the baking of bread was even more efficient than before, and the benefit to the baker's customers increased—more quality for less expense.

And so capitalism transformed the world. Everyone who trades benefits, and the retained capital buys machines and processes that improve productivity, so the benefits continue.

Then Industrialization Perfected the Capitalism Model (and Destroyed the Culture, Replacing It with Something Shinier)

Capitalism was refined and condensed and iterated until it became a monster.

The industrialist not only wants to make ever-more-productive trades, driving quality up and costs down, but insists on changing two things that have never been changed at a mammoth, world-wide scale before.

Change the culture. The industrialist is big enough and powerful enough and profitable enough that he can act like royalty. He doesn't issue decrees by royal fiat; he does it with advertising and lobbying and by offering a huge carrot to anyone who complies.

Thanks to industrialists and their bountiful profits, our definition of success was changed. The nature of education was changed. The very way we spent our time and our resources was transformed by mass advertising, mass schooling, and mass production.

The industrialist lobbied to build his plant on the river and then filled it with effluent. He opened the doors to repetitive jobs and the numbing hierarchy of middle management. He demanded a seat at every table—a voice in how we ran our government, our schools, our science, and our spiritual organizations. But it was all okay, because the productivity he created made us relatively wealthy, fed our children, and delivered medical care as well. Industrialism brought hospitals and CD players and the Egg McMuffin. What could be bad about that?

The change in culture went further than most expected. Another change followed. . . .

Change our dreams. The overwhelming impact of more than a century of cultural indoctrination can't be overstated. We have embraced industrial propaganda with such enthusiasm that we have changed the very nature of our dreams.

Being a human today means more wealth, better health, and the leverage to influence others. But it also is a fundamentally different existence from the one we had for millennia before this.

The industrialist needs you to dream about security and the benefits of compliance. The industrialist works to sell you on a cycle of consumption (which requires more compliance). And the industrialist benefits from our dream of moving up the corporate ladder, *his* ladder.

Capitalism is driven by failure, the failure of new ideas to catch on or the failure of the organization that fails when it is beaten by new competition. Industrialization is about eliminating the risk of failure, about maintaining the status quo, and about cementing power. "Too big to fail" is the goal of every industrialist, but "too big to fail" means that capitalism is no longer functioning.

It's Not Personal; It Can't Be

After nearly a century of effort, the industrial system has created the worker-proof factory.

It's okay if the person assembling your Domino's pizza or Apple iPhone doesn't care. The system cares. The system measures every movement, every bit of output, so all the tolerances are in order.

It's okay if the person at the bank doesn't care—the real work is done by an ATM or a spreadsheet. We've systematized and mechanized every step of every process.

By eliminating "personal" from frontline labor, the industrial system ensures that it can both maintain quality and use ever-cheaper (and ever-fewer) workers.

Thinking About Pink Slime

After Eldon Roth invented "boneless lean beef trimmings," the invention seemed like an obvious move by the industrialized meat-producing system. Mix a refined chemical (ammonium hydroxide) with the last bit of fat and scrap that's left over after slaughtering a cow. Heat it, spin it, refine it again, and you can add this soupy mixture to ground beef, cutting the cost to the consumer.

This was only the most recent advance in the industrialization of the production of food. From the way cows are raised and fed to the way the work is mechanized and scaled, every step of the process is optimized for speed, cost, and efficiency. Without many of these advances, we'd have to either change our lifestyle or run out of food.

At some point, though, many people decided that pink slime was a bridge too far. At some point, consumers said that the savings of an extra two cents a pound wasn't worth the story we'd have to tell ourselves about what we were eating and how it was made.

Industrialists have always been cheered as they raced to create more efficiencies, more scalability, and more speed. But both the economics and the ethics of the last bit of industrialization don't really scale. We can't make it much faster or much cheaper, and dehumanizing everything we touch has a cost.

Industrialism Has Spread

The media are industrialized now, with no one in the chain taking responsibility for what's reported, with fewer independent voices, and with a predictable sameness designed to make the system ever more efficient.

Organized religions have followed this model as well. So have big-time sports. Powerful industrialists make decisions about what leads to long-term dominance and stability, as opposed to celebrating risk and humanity. These decisions change what we watch, how we live, and what we dream about.

The industrial model of command and control and the avoidance of failure now permeate every corner of the culture.

The Man's Dancing Monkey

Former actor, former comedian, former felon (for lighting Jay Leno's couch on fire) Bobcat Goldthwait writes:

> I have been a game-show host, a talking puppet, and a Happy Meal toy. My acting has been dubbed into more languages than I can name. I cashed huge studio checks and got

flown around the world. And I was miserable the entire time. Seriously—being the man's dancing monkey was . . . horrible. I'm not bitter about it now (no, really), because it's behind me. I love my life now. But it took me almost 30 years to get here.

Just because you're winning a game doesn't mean it's a good game.

Snapshots from the Industrial Age: Is Conformity the Best We Can Do?

The industrial age that is fading all around us was built around productivity. The reason for all of it—for the exodus from farms, for the growth of mass media, for the standardization of schools, roads, and the marketplace—was that mass production, inter-changeable parts, and the mass market were insanely productive.

Simple handmade elements of life, like bread, were industrialized. Industrial bread was cheaper, faster, and easy to turn a profit on. As a result, flour turned white, distribution channels lengthened, and the personality of the baker was isolated from that of his bread. Wonder Bread is an artifact of its time, a representation of the might of the system, regardless of its output.

———

In 1919 C. A. Adams, of both Harvard University and the U.S. Bureau of Standards, wrote:

> Most of us talk of standardization in a vague way, usually having in mind some particular corner of the subject, but without full realization of the comprehensiveness of the word,

of the magnitude and importance of the field covered, or that the coöperation without which our modern society would be impossible would in turn be impossible without a large measure of standardization. *It might almost be said that the degree of standardization in any nation is a measure of its civilization*, certainly in the material sense of the word [emphasis added].

———

J. Edgar Hoover industrialized the FBI, turning law enforcement from a handmade local enterprise into a systemized, standardized operation.

George Anders reports that Hoover (who ran the FBI for forty-eight years) built an organization of more than 8,000 agents. The roster included no women and fewer than 150 black, Asian, or Latino men. In one astonishing display of top-down conformity, Hoover visited the FBI training academy and told one of his lieutenants that he didn't like seeing "pinheads" in the ranks. The FBI then opened the locker of each trainee, measured his hat size, and kicked out three candidates because they had hat sizes smaller than seven.

———

In 1947 a family-owned contractor and builder invented the modern suburb. Levittown was a mass-produced, industrialized, optimized subdivision, a place where houses could be built with efficiency (Levitt & Sons finished thirty houses a day). Demand for housing, cheap, in mass, with built-in societal approval, led the first phase of Levittown to become a complete success in less than two days.

Conformity was easier, safer, and cheaper than diversity.

———

Writing a résumé isn't particularly difficult. The layout, typography, and paper stock are standardized.

The purpose of the résumé hasn't changed, but the way it's processed has. It's not unusual for a big company to get more than two thousand résumés a day, and they're not read by a person; they're read by a computer.

The computer is looking for signals—signals of conformity. Did you go to a famous college, did you work for a well-known brand, did you have a title that matches what the company thinks it's looking for?

There's so much mass, there are so many people, how can the system process the masses any other way?

———

College has changed. The founders of Harvard and Oxford would have trouble recognizing the industrialized institutions we have today.

They had no choice but to standardize and industrialize. As soon as college's role was transformed from that of divinity school and refuge for scholars to that of finishing school for the elite and anyone seeking a position of influence, the schools had little choice but to establish a scalable curriculum, one that could be industrialized enough to handle the demand.

College started as *universitas magistrorum et scholarium*—a community of masters and scholars. It was a refuge; it was a place you went to get lost in ideas, to discover and wander, and to plot a course as an academic.

Today it's a place you go to exchange a lifetime of debt for credit hours, a degree, and maybe a good job. So many people attend (as a percentage of the population, college attendance is ten times what it was a few generations ago) that the universities have no choice but to standardize degree requirements, test, and measure as they compete to make their colleges ever more famous via faux rankings and football games.

> Everybody is a genius. But if you judge a fish by its ability to climb a tree, it will live its whole life believing that it is stupid.
>
> —Albert Einstein

Standardization in the industrial age was not a choice. It was impossible to industrialize without it.

Originality and art in the connected age are not a choice, either. It's impossible to do the work before us without them. It's impossible to connect without art.

The old safety zone is dead. Long live the new safety zone.

Sacrifices Before Moloch

> Moloch whose mind is pure machinery! Moloch whose blood is running money! Moloch whose fingers are ten armies! Moloch whose breast is a cannibal dynamo! Moloch whose ear is a smoking tomb!
>
> —Allen Ginsberg, "Howl"

The system demanded a high price for its promises of safety and reassurance and gimcracks. It demanded that we give up our voices and accept different, lesser dreams. We traded debt for an SUV, sure, but we also traded independent thought and the ability to stand up and say, "Look what I did."

The new, connected economy demands different sacrifices and offers a different sort of safety zone. In this new safety zone, we are surrounded not by the mass market but by the weird, by the few who care deeply about what we're capable of. This economy demands that we spin the log ever faster—doing not the work of making the same widget faster and cheaper in a race to the bottom but the work of connecting and entertaining and amazing with our most vivid dreams.

Not for Everyone

The weird are the people outside the normal zone. The normal distribution ruled the lives of the last four generations. It was the curve that defined the mass market, that showed where efficiency of marketing and manufacturing lay.

DVD players cost eighty dollars because they're cheap to make when everyone wants one. Walmart moves into a town and the masses shop there, enabling huge selection and cheaper prices. Mass marketing is efficient.

The Internet and the connection economy turn the economics of mass on its head. It's now cheaper and more efficient to make edgy, amazing products for the weird edge cases (who are listening and talking and who care) than it is to push yet another average product onto the already overloaded average people in the middle of the curve.

Better Safe Than Sorry

In the industrial age, the age of standardization and interchangeable parts, it's all about being safe.

The system is so valuable, the processes so polished, that safe guarantees productivity and profits.

Keep it moving. Keep it efficient. Keep it reliable.

Better Sorry Than Safe

And that's the heart of the argument about our future.

In the industrial age, there's no question that it was better to be safe than sorry. Better to close an airport hours before the storm hit than to risk having a plane get stuck somewhere.

As the power and impact of the industrial age peak and inevitably shrink, safe isn't helpful. We can be as safe as possible and it's not going to generate growth, it's not going to take advantage of the myriad connections we can now make, and it's certainly not going to benefit you. The representatives of Moloch will pick someone even safer than you, guaranteed.

No, the only path left veers away from safe and heads straight for sorry.

Sorry?

Yes, the sorry of vulnerability and unpredictability and repeated failure. Combined with the joy of connection, breakthroughs, and humanity.

The Right Answer

> He felt his whole body hot and confused in a moment.
> What was the right answer to the question? He had given
> two and still Wells laughed. But Wells *must* know the
> right answer for he was in third of grammar.
>
> —James Joyce, *A Portrait of the Artist as a Young Man*

The search for the right answer is the enemy of art. The right answer belongs to the productivity-minded industrialists, to Taylor and the denizens of Scientific Management.

Icarus was told not to fly too high and not to fly too low. But what's the right altitude? Where's the map, where's the safe middle?

Art has no right answer. The best we can hope for is an interesting answer.

But Is It Even Possible?

Do you have the right stuff? The ability to do important work, to make art, to challenge the status quo? What if it is for other people and not for you?

Malcolm Gladwell famously reported that most NHL players are born in January, February, or March. The reason, it turns out, is that when you're eight years old, being nine months older than the other kids is a huge advantage. That advantage gets you a spot on the traveling team, more ice time, and better coaching, and it compounds. In some ways, certain Canadian boys are born to play hockey, if born means the right country and the right birthday.

If your goal was to be in the NHL one day, then your zodiac sign matters a great deal.

Fortunately for the rest of us (all of us?), art is not only possible; it's inevitable if we allow it to happen.

There are so many places that art and connection are needed, so many avenues that are open, so many opportunities, that no one is boxed out. It's not about whether we have what it takes; it's about whether we choose to pursue it.

Of course it's difficult to overcome a lifetime of education (and brainwashing). New habits will have to be created, and new expectations to go with them. But the astonishing news is that for the first time in recorded history, it matters not so much where you're born or what your DNA says about you—the connection economy is waiting for you to step forward, with only the resistance to hold you back.

Have patience with everything unresolved in your heart and try to love the questions themselves.

—Rainer Maria Rilke

Hope, the Lottery, and Compliance

Hope is an essential part of the human condition. Without hope, we wither and perish.

But how to create hope in an industrialized society, in an economy where compliance on the assembly line is the best way to produce productivity? Our economy has become a giant lottery.

Perhaps you'll get picked to be on *American Idol*. Perhaps you'll sue someone and get a windfall. Perhaps you'll be the one who gets promoted to partner as a result of all your hard work (but maybe you won't).

We celebrate the *Forbes* 400 and the masters of the universe and the lucky few who have won the corporate lottery, because secretly we are celebrating our chances of winning the lottery as well. Like most lotteries, this is a loser's game, with the odds against us. What appears to be a meritocracy is actually a rigged game and a wheel of fortune.

The marketers feed the population a constant stream of products that are apparently worth buying. The broadcasters mix the ads with amusements and diversions. Sit quietly, do what you're told, and perhaps, one day, you'll get out of debt and be a winner.

The alternative, which is the independent creation of art, doesn't happen overnight. You don't win the art lottery and get picked and suddenly find all doors open and receptive to your vision and generosity and talent. No, the commitment to art is the return of an ancient habit, one that was relentlessly extinguished for a long time.

We can't suddenly quit a job and then race to find a form of art that will pay off before the next mortgage payment is due. Creating art is a habit, one that we practice daily or hourly until we get good at it.

Art isn't about the rush of victory that comes from being picked. Nor does it involve compliance. Art in the postindustrial age is a lifelong habit, a stepwise process that incrementally allows us to create even more art.

The Assets That Matter

Successful organizations have realized that they are no longer in the business of coining slogans, running catchy ads, and optimizing their supply chains to cut costs.

And freelancers and soloists have discovered that doing a good job for a fair price is no longer sufficient to guarantee success. Good work is easier to find than ever before.

What matters now:

- Trust
- Permission
- Remarkability
- Leadership
- Stories that spread
- Humanity: connection, compassion, and humility

And here's the thing: All six of these are the result of successful work by artists. These assets aren't generated by external strategies and MBAs and positioning memos. These are the results of internal trauma, of brave decisions and the willingness to live with dignity.

They are about standing out, not fitting in, about inventing, not duplicating.

TRUST AND PERMISSION: In a marketplace that's open to just about anyone, the only people we hear are the people we choose to hear. Media is cheap, sure, but attention is filtered, and it's virtually impossible to be heard unless the consumer gives us the ability to be heard. The more valuable someone's attention is, the harder it is to earn.

And who gets heard?

Why would someone listen to the prankster or the shyster or the huckster? No, we choose to listen to those we trust. We do business with and donate to those who have earned our attention. We seek out people who tell us stories that resonate, we listen to those stories, and we engage with those people or businesses who delight or reassure or surprise in a positive way.

And all of those behaviors are the acts of people, not machines. We embrace the humanity in those around us, particularly as the rest of the world appears to become less human and more cold. Who will you miss? That is who you are listening to.

REMARKABILITY: The same bias toward art exists in the way we choose which ideas we'll share with our friends and colleagues. No one talks about the boring, the predictable, or the safe. We don't risk interactions in order to spread the word about something obvious or trite.

The remarkable is almost always new and untested, fresh and risky.

LEADERSHIP: Management is almost diametrically opposed to leadership. Management is about generating yesterday's results, but a little faster or a little more cheaply. We know how to manage the world—we relentlessly seek to cut costs and to limit variation, while we exalt obedience.

Leadership, though, is a whole other game. Leadership puts the leader on the line. No manual, no rule book, no überleader to point the finger at when things go wrong. If you ask someone for the rule book on how to lead, you're secretly wishing to be a manager.

Leaders are vulnerable, not controlling, and they are taking us to a new place, not to the place of cheap, fast, compliant safety.

STORIES THAT SPREAD: The next asset that makes the new economy work is the story that spreads. Before the revolution, in a world of limited choice, shelf space mattered a great deal. You could buy your way onto the store shelf, or you could be the only one on the ballot, or you could use a connection to get your résumé in front of the hiring guy. In a world of abundant choice, though, none of these tactics is effective. The chooser has too many alternatives, there's too much clutter, and the scarce resources are attention and trust, not shelf space. This situation is tough for many, because attention and trust must be earned, not acquired.

More difficult still is the magic of the story that resonates. After trust is earned and your work is seen, only a fraction of it is magical enough to be worth spreading. Again, this magic is the work of the human artist, not the corporate machine.

HUMANITY: We don't worship industrial the way we used to. We seek out human originality and caring instead. When price and availability are no longer sufficient advantages (because everything is available and the price is no longer news), then what we are drawn to is the vulnerability and transparency that bring us together, that turn the "other" into one of us.

For a long time to come the masses will still clamor for cheap and obvious and reliable. But the people you seek to lead, the people who are helping to define the next thing and the interesting frontier, these people want your humanity, not your discounts.

All of these assets, rolled into one, provide the foundation for the change maker of the future. And that individual (or the team that person leads) has no choice but to build these assets with novelty, with a fresh approach to an old problem, with a human touch that is worth talking about.

Holding back is so close to stealing.

—Neil Young

There's No Business Like Show Business

As Ethel Merman sang about the unhappiness of the workingman, they "get paid for what they do, but no applause."

Not the applause from the seats of the theater, of course, but the applause that comes from a personal connection with someone who is pleased with the workingman's work, delighted with his decisions, and grateful for his effort.

If what you've done is what you've been ordered to do, then the labor doesn't seem to belong to you. The craftsman and the artist say, "Here, I made this." The workingman is asked to follow instructions.

The extraordinary thing about our revolution is that it is turning most business into show business. Even nonbusiness projects, from school to fund-raising, feel more like show business than we've seen before.

The sale of a box of cookies, for example, is no longer a simple transaction about money in exchange for sweet crunch. The story of the Girl Scout cookie or the fancy packaging of the Tate's cookie or the gluten-free wonder of the local bakery's homemade cookie— this is show business, not a cookie.

The doctor who spends 25 percent of his time writing articles, blogging, or appearing on television to tell the story of his new procedure is certainly not practicing medicine the way his father would recognize.

The hotel concierge, the talent agent, and the car mechanic are all discovering that when they move from task to show, from spec to connection, they are adding far more value than ever before.

For the first time in history, most of us have the chance to decide what to do next, what to make, how to deliver it. Most of us won't take that chance, but it's there.

Connection Requires Emotional Labor

If you want access to my attention, my gratitude, and my soul, you will earn it with your emotional labor. The last economy was built on the nonscalable hard work of physical labor. *Physical* because it involved our muscles or the repetitive work of our intellect. *Nonscalable* because a little more effort got only a little more pay. Nonscalable because a lot more effort was impossible.

This economy is built on art, the art that is created by emotional labor, by bringing risk and joy and fear and love to the table.

Emotional labor scales in that *a little more emotional labor is often worth a lot.*

Connection between people is always the result of emotional labor, not physical labor. The assets of trust and leadership and conversation can come only from the difficult work of creating personal art.

Easier to say than to do.

Most of us nod, acknowledge the need to create these bonds of connection through the very frightening and draining work of emotional labor, and then immediately head back to the old comfort zone of physical labor and following instructions. Because it feels less risky and comes with deniability.

The Heart of the Connection Economy

I don't care how many friends you have on Facebook or how many followers you have on Twitter. Those are not actual friends or truly followers.

I care about how much people will miss you if you're not back here again tomorrow.

Connection involves a complex swap of information, expectation, and culture. It involves opening ourselves to others, creating vulnerable moments that frighten us. It requires humanity and generosity, not the rearranging of digital bits.

The swap means that it's no longer completely up to us; it's a partnership, not an announcement. When we give up control over the outcome of our interactions, we allow others to connect with us and with one another.

The Abundance of the Connection Economy

As the final days of the industrial age roll around, we are seeing the core assets of the economy replaced by something new. Actually, it's something old, but on a huge scale.

The industrial age was about scarcity. Everything that built our culture, improved our productivity, and defined our lives involved the chasing of scarce items.

The connection economy, on the other hand, embraces abundance. No, we don't have an endless supply of the resources we used to trade and covet. No, we certainly don't have a surplus of time, either. But we do have an abundance of choice, an abundance of connection, and an abundance of knowledge.

We know more people, have access to more resources, and can leverage our skills more quickly and at a higher level than ever before.

This abundance leads to two races. The race to the bottom is the Internet-fueled challenge to lower prices, find cheaper labor, and deliver more for less.

The other race is the race to the top, the opportunity to be the one they can't live without, to become a linchpin (whom we would miss if he didn't show up). The race to the top focuses on *delivering more for more*. It embraces the weird passions of those with the resources to make choices, and it rewards originality, remarkability, and art.

The connection economy continues to gain traction because connections scale, information begets more information, and influence accrues to those who create this abundance. As connections scale, these connections paradoxically make it easier for others to connect as well, because anyone with talent or passion can leverage the networks created by connection to increase her impact.

Just as the phone network becomes more valuable when more phones are connected (scarcity is the enemy of value in a network), the connection economy becomes more valuable as we scale it.

Friends bring us more friends. A reputation brings us a chance to build a better reputation. Access to information encourages us to seek ever more information. The connections in our life multiply and increase in value. Our stuff, on the other hand, merely gets cheaper over time.

The Opportunity to Say "Go"

At the same time that the connection economy has destroyed the value of the status quo, it has created an opportunity for anyone who chooses to connect. Connection isn't created by expensive factories or by large workforces, so the barrier to individual advancement is destroyed. It's not what you've got; it's how brave you're prepared to be.

Connections can be made online or off, and they have value. Instead of relying on gatekeepers to block the way of those without the right degree, the right parents, or the right connections, the connection economy works horizontally—allowing anyone to stand up and make an offer.

Of course, most of those offers, most of that art, are rejected. The connection economy offers tremendous value to those who connect, but that doesn't mean connection is guaranteed. It's valuable because it's so scarce. Fortunately, the cost of finding out what will connect is lower than you might imagine, and the chance to do it again is easily taken.

So start.

Doing Less Versus Doing More

The laborer in the world of physical labor seeks opportunities to do a little bit less. Since physical labor rarely scales, a little bit less for the same pay is a great deal for the one doing the labor, a shortcut worth seeking out.

Physical labor struggles to produce more, because we can move our hands only so quickly, fill out only so many forms per hour, answer just that many calls a day. Physical labor doesn't scale because more hours for more output stops working after we run out of hours.

The laborer in the world of connection and art embraces the opportunity to do a little bit more, not less. Since emotional labor scales so dramatically, the ability to bring a little more to the table is the chance of a lifetime. "A little more" compounds, because ideas spread. A little more compounds because in a connected economy, word spreads and people flock to the art that means more.

You don't need more activity; you have to dig deeper instead.

Connection belongs to those who "get to" instead of "have to."

The Kitten and the Monkey

When a kitten gets into trouble, his mother comes and gently picks him up by the neck, rescuing him and taking him to safety.

A baby monkey, on the other hand, has no choice but to grab onto the back of his mother if he wants to make an escape.

One is rescued; the other rescues himself.

In Japanese, *tariki* is the name for choosing to be helped, seeking a higher authority to select you, move you forward, and endorse you. *Tariki* is the helpless kitten. *Jiriki*, alternatively, is self-selection, self-authorized art. *Jiriki* is the monkey who saves himself.

The industrial economy insisted on *tariki*. It treated workers like kittens and abhorred anyone who would add innovation or individualism to the system.

The connection economy opens the door for *jiriki*.

Pick Yourself

Authority?

You want the authority to create, to be noticed, and to make a difference? You're waiting for permission to stand up and speak up and ship?

Sorry. There's no authority left.

Oprah has left the building. She can't choose you to be on her show because her show is gone.

YouTube wants you to have your own show now, but they're not going to call you.

Dick Clark has left the building. He's not going to be able to get you a record deal or a TV gig because he and his show are long gone. iTunes and a hundred other outlets want you to have your own gig, but they're not going to call you, either.

Neither is Rodney Dangerfield or the head of programming at Comedy Central. Louis C.K. has famously proven that he doesn't need the tyranny of the booker—he booked himself. Marc Maron didn't wait to be cast on *Saturday Night Live*—he started his own podcast and earned a million listeners.

Our cultural instinct is to wait to get picked. To seek out the permission, authority, and safety that come from a publisher or a talk-show host or even a blogger who says, "I pick you."

Once you reject that impulse and realize that no one is going to select you—that Prince Charming has chosen another house in his search for Cinderella—then you can actually get to work.

The myth that the CEO is going to discover you and nurture you and ask you to join her for lunch is just that, a Hollywood myth.

Once you understand that there are problems waiting to be solved, once you realize that you have all the tools and all the permission you need, then opportunities to contribute abound. The opportunity is not to have your résumé picked from the pile but to lead.

When we take responsibility and eagerly give credit, doors open. When we grab a microphone and speak up, we're a step closer to doing the work we're able to do.

Most of all, when we buckle down, confront the lizard brain, and ship our best work, we're becoming the artists we are capable of becoming.

No one is going to pick you. Pick yourself.

How much responsibility are you willing to take before it's given to you?

The Math of Self-Selection

We've all seen the music industry fall apart. Even if you're not a musician, it's worth considering the implications when the connection revolution permits a musician to bypass the label and pick herself.

According to Jeff Price at TuneCore, the math of before and after the revolution in the music business looks like this:

Before the revolution:

Virtually all musicians aren't picked by a label and are invisible nonentities.

Of those who are picked, 98 percent fail in the marketplace.

Of the remaining 2 percent, less than half a percent ever receive a single royalty check as a result of their recorded music. Ever.

So we have a world where the odds of being signed are close to zero and the odds of getting a check as a result of your sales, even if you are signed, is even closer to zero.

After the revolution:

A musician who sells two (two!) copies of a song on iTunes makes more money than she would have earned from a record label for selling an entire CD for seventeen dollars.

There are more musicians making more music being heard by more people and earning more money than ever before.

Now, multiply what happened to music by a million. Multiply it by consulting, coaching, and design. Multiply it by manufacturing, speaking, and nonprofits. Multiply it by whatever it is you care enough to do.

That's what *after* looks like.

Someone Else's Dreams

A true story: Sarah loves to perform musical theater. She loves the energy of being onstage, the flow of being in the moment, the *frisson* of feeling the rest of the troupe in sync as she moves.

And yet . . .

And yet Sarah spends 98 percent of her time trying to be picked. She goes to casting calls, sends out head shots, follows every lead. And then she deals with the heartbreak of rejection, of being hassled or seeing her skills disrespected.

All so she can be in front of the right audience.

Which audience is the right one? The audience of critics and theatergoers and the rest of the authorities. After all, that's what musical theater is. Its pinnacle is at City Center and on Broadway, and if she's lucky, Ben Brantley from the *Times* will be there and

Baryshnikov will be in the audience and the reviewers will like her show and she might even get mentioned. All so she can do it again.

This is her agent's dream and the casting agency's dream and the director's dream and the theater owner's dream and the producer's dream. It's a dream that gives money to those who want to put on the next show and gives power to the professionals who can give the nod and, yes, pick someone.

But wait. Sarah's joy is in the dance. It's in the moment. Her joy is in creating flow.

Strip away all the cruft and what we see is that virtually none of the demeaning work she does to be picked is necessary. What if she performs for the "wrong" audience? What if she follows Banksy's lead and takes her art to the street? What if she performs in classrooms or prisons or for some (sorry to use air quotes here) "lesser" audience?

Who decided that a performance in alternative venues for alternative audiences wasn't legitimate dance, couldn't be real art, didn't create as much joy, wasn't as real? Who decided that Sarah couldn't be an impresario and pick herself?

The people who pick decided that.

When Sarah chooses herself, when she makes her own art on her own terms, two things happen: She unlocks her ability to make an impact, removing all the excuses between her current place and the art she wants to make. And she exposes herself, because now it's her decision to perform, not the casting director's. It's her repertoire that's being judged, not the dramaturge's. And most of all, it's her choice of audience, not the choice of some official, suit-wearing authority figure.

The birth of the connection revolution opened the door for this sort of choice making. Now, just a few years into the revolution, it *demands* choice making.

Not Even Once?

If you've spent your life hewing to the industrialist's set of rules, it's easy to convince yourself that you don't have what it takes to make art. Inventing rules isn't your thing; following them is. You don't see yourself as the person who takes responsibility; instead you might be the one who is given authority.

About which I'd ask, "Even once?"

Have you ever performed a generous, unexpected act? Solved a problem in a new and interesting way? Seen something others didn't see? Spoken up when something needed to be said?

If just one time you've made a connection, bridged a gap, or done something about an issue you care about, then yes, you're an artist. Maybe not all the time, or even most of the time, but yes, you've done it and you can do it again.

All that's left is to figure out how to create habits so you can do it more often.

Stop Trying to Put My Round Job in Your Square Hole

Valve is a cutting-edge computer game company, responsible for the successful Steam platform. Their future depends on hiring artistic and fearless employees willing to advance and change the state of the art.

To encourage this, they've completely rebuilt their corporate culture, famously publishing an employee handbook that turns just about every corporate convention upside down. Consider this excerpt:

What if I Screw Up?

Nobody has ever been fired at Valve for making a mistake. It wouldn't make sense for us to operate that way. Providing the freedom to fail is an important trait of the company—we couldn't expect so much of individuals if we also penalized people for errors. Even expensive mistakes, or ones which result in a very public failure, are genuinely looked at as opportunities to learn. We can always repair the mistake or make up for it.

And yet. And yet Valve's employees still need to be reassured and pushed and cajoled into stepping up and doing important work. A hundred years of industrial brainwashing and a hundred years of cultural pressure make it hard for new employees to take promises like this at face value and hard for long-term employees to truly understand how gutsy the company wants them to be.

At nonprofits, political campaigns, and cutting-edge companies, this disconnect happens daily. Someone realizes how important human risk taking and art are, yet employees who have bought into the Icarus Deception perversely fight to keep the system the way it used to be.

I'm under no illusions that a short book is going to change your biases completely. What I'm hoping I might do is get under your skin enough that you'll ask yourself some hard questions about why you're not achieving as much as you would like (and why you're not as happy as you'd like to be).

The connection economy has revolutionized what it means to go to work. It has given you all the tools necessary to pick yourself. And it's not a trap. It's an opportunity.

Why So Many Entrepreneurs Have Dyslexia and ADHD

Julie Logan at the Cass Business School found that entrepreneurs are three times more likely than the general public to have dyslexia. And many entrepreneurs credit their ADHD with giving them an edge in making their businesses successful.

I'm not sure it's because their mental differences give them a performance edge. It's not like there's a secret code that only dyslexics can read. No, I think it's because their outlier tendencies made it clear to them early on that they would be less likely to be picked. Less likely to be at the top of their class or chosen by the fancy college or recruited by P&G. Precisely because they didn't fit in, they had little choice but to pick themselves.

And once that choice is made, it becomes a habit.

Do Not Waste a Moment

The door to art and connection is open, but we have no idea for how long.

Every day on the other side of the door is better than a day on this side. Every moment that we wait, biding our time, waiting for the perfect opportunity, is a moment wasted and, worse, a door that closes, possibly not to open again for a long time to come.

Adrienne Rich wrote, "The door itself makes no promises. It is only a door." Behind that door, though, lies connection and the possibilities that come from having people who want to hear what you have to say, who look forward to having you make what you choose to make.

What's certain about this door is that the frustration you feel about the dying industrial economy is only going to increase, and connection and art offer a path that is, at the very least, more interesting.

What I Mean by "Connection"

Overlooked in all the hoopla about YouTube videos, liking, friending, and flat-belly diets is the truth about the Internet: It is starting to deliver something that people can't get enough of.

Once a street has two or three pizza places, it gets pretty hard to sell more pizza. Hunger doesn't scale (fortunately). But connection? We're insatiable consumers of connection.

Our basic human need to be understood, respected, and missed when we're gone doesn't get satisfied easily. As a result, when genuine connection is offered, it's often taken.

We have easily agreed-upon definitions for the quality standards of mechanical devices, the tolerance requirements of machined components, or the way to measure the distortion of an amplifier or the efficiency of a certain kind of water filter. But we have no good way to measure connection or even talk about it. Since connection is an essential element of art, it's worth a moment or two to explore this essential but elusive concept.

Connection begins with dignity.

We're surrounded by servants. Flight attendants, waiters, car valets, street sweepers, the guy behind the counter at the post office. Each of these people is serving us in exchange for pay.

And the world moves so fast and we're so spoiled and the airline seats cost so much and we're so busy and we're having such a bad day and . . . it's easy to ignore them. It's easy to treat people as invisible, as long as we get what we want.

If the line is long or the prices are high or the clerk just doesn't know where to put us since the hotel is sold out, it's easy to have a tantrum and to push ourselves away from the interaction and, worse, away from the person who just sought to serve us.

The alternative is an interaction that creates a connection instead of destroying it. Where is the eye contact? Where is the dignity that comes from recognizing another?

When we humanize the person at the other end of the counter or the phone or the Internet, we grant them something precious—personhood. When we treat the people around us with dignity, we create an entirely different platform for the words we utter and the plans we make.

It's impossible to connect with a device or an automaton. It's worthwhile to connect with a person, to someone we have granted the dignity that she deserves.

Industrialization Destroys Itself When It Refuses Dignity

A hundred years of faith in the industrial system changed our culture. But now, just as the financial rewards of the industrial system are faltering, many people are realizing that the deal was a sour one.

When we write a check to charity instead of looking the needy in the eye, we have helped their physical needs but shortchanged their humanity. When we demand that our workers engage in a race to the bottom with any country willing to work faster and more robotically, we take something away from the people we work with. And when we shrug and invoke Ayn Rand or the invisible hand of the market, we are trading our humanity for some extra stuff in the garage or a bigger addition to our house.

If the object of the game we are playing was merely to make the most stuff for the least money, there would be no issue with any of this. But the artist understands that there's a different game being played, one that focuses on connection. The safe place is not the sinecure where we get a good wage from the industrialist. That's eroding fast. The new safe place requires us to look others in the eye and see them, truly see them.

Connection Is the Outcome of Art

How much connection did you just make? That's one way to measure whether or not the work you did made a difference.

When you make a daring comment at a meeting, how many people are able to leverage it or respond to it or work with it?

When you produce a video or an app or an idea and it spreads from person to person, it creates a bridge that connects us.

When more people visit your farm stand because they can't get enough of the way you and your team engage, you are bringing excitement and fellowship to a place where it didn't used to live.

Boring and safe rarely lead to connection. Connection happens when humanity asserts itself. If there's no connection, if the links aren't made, then no art occurred.

The Perverse Irony of the Argument

People pick up business books (like this one) looking for a map. They pay attention in school because they want certainty: the certainty of a good grade, a good job, a good career. We transformed school from a place of inquiry into a facility optimized for meeting standards. This is something the industrial age taught us—that there are answers and that you need the answers in order to succeed. Memorize enough answers and you're set.

The connection economy asks you to turn all of that upside down, to not want or need or seek a map. Your instinct to search for a sinecure (that thing that was a safety zone and is now merely a comfort zone) is proof that you've been brainwashed.

The brainwashing is subtle: It doesn't change our basic human need for safety. In fact, it uses that need to convince us that the safe place (the comfort zone) is the place where we do what we know and do what we're told.

Whenever you feel the pull toward compliance and obedience, feel it for what it is—a reminder of the way you've been trained, not a sensible or rational approach to the opportunity in front of you.

So here's a book that instead of giving you a map (which business books are supposed to do), refuses to.

The most rational thing to do is the irrational work of art.

Seek out questions, not answers.

The Economy Isn't Broken; It's Different

The inputs and outputs of the connection economy are very different, and our traditional measurements of value and productivity are failing us. Worse, the good jobs that were the backbone of our culture (steady, white-collar jobs where respect and high pay were coupled with credentials and obedience) are disappearing fast, leaving angst in their wake.

Ask a doctor what's happened to her practice in the last ten years, or go visit the empty factory down the street that's been moved to a place where people work more cheaply. . . .

Can we really produce more shiny objects to delight an ever-growing population? Can we give the people who already have endless stuff even more pleasure by giving them even more stuff?

The economy we live in today is very different from the one our parents grew up in. We have a surplus of choice, a surplus of quality, a surplus of entertainments to choose from. We have big-box stores and big-box storage units and big-box debt.

But we're still lonely.

And we're still bored.

The connection economy works because it focuses on the lonely and the bored. It works because it embraces the individual, not the mob; the weird, not the normal.

The connection economy revolves around the linchpin, the artist we can't live without, the individual who chooses to do work that matters, because without her, why connect?

Fighting Numbness

It's entirely possible to use the productivity of our economy to try to insulate ourselves from the pain of uncertainty. We can demand that our politicians deliver steady work in a factory setting, and we can scream for fair pay in exchange for our mind-numbing labor. We can fight to go back to trading money for numbness.

The best part of being human doesn't seek out numbness. And

today, right now, our economy rewards us for being artists, no longer hypnotized, no longer cogs, no longer insulated from one another and ourselves.

We have the opportunity to go backward if we choose. We can try to prop up failing industries, legislate and calcify our way into the notion of a day's work for a day's pay.

Or we can choose a different path, one where we willingly expose ourselves to the apparent insecurity and risk of emotional labor, of creating breakthroughs instead of reliably lowering the price of the banal.

> To be yourself in a world that is constantly trying to make you something else is the greatest accomplishment.
>
> —Ralph Waldo Emerson

The Itch

We evolved to desire safety. We seek out security. We want a hiding place, a dependable future, something we can count on.

And yet.

And yet the itch comes back. The itch to provoke or risk or stand up. The itch to test, to prod, and to stand out.

For some the itch is nothing but a slight buzz, something causing discomfort in an otherwise bland day. For others the itch becomes so overwhelming that it overtakes them, dominating their day and putting their souls on the line.

The itch has always been there, of course. It's been there for generations, provoking Copernicus and Biko, King and Gandhi. It is responsible for our inventions and our discoveries and our epic failures. The itch led us to war and to electricity, to Ionesco and to Zander.

Most of the time, for most of us, it's merely in the background. Culturally, we're taught to avoid scratching the itch, to be reasonable and focused and to plan for an unreliable future. Take what you can get, protect it, and keep your head down.

Recently, though, our economy has lined up with the human instinct to see what happens. Make a list of those whom we seek out, whom we pay well, who get to achieve their goals, attract our attention, and make things. They are the artists who never know what will work, who make something and see what happens.

See what happens. Uncertain, but worth it.

Who Will Teach Bravery?

There's not much controversy about teaching reading or spelling or math. It's assumed that we ought to have systems in place to establish cultural norms and behavior and a passing knowledge of current events.

But who is worried about creating a new generation of brave artists? Brave because artists take leaps, brave because artists fail— the willingness to fail and then do it again is the cost of doing art, and for some, it becomes part of the reason to do art.

Are we avoiding this vital work because it's difficult to teach or, more likely, because the industrialists who run our system would rather we were docile?

Brainwashed from an Early Age

The notion that an organization can teach anything at all is a relatively new one.

Traditionally, society assumed that artists, singers, artisans, writers, scientists, and alchemists would find their calling, then find a mentor, and *then* learn their craft. It was absurd to think that you'd take people off the street, teach them to do science or to sing, and persist at that teaching long enough for them to get excited about it.

Now that we've built an industrial solution for teaching in bulk, we've seduced ourselves into believing that the only thing that can be taught is the way to get high SAT scores.

We shouldn't be buying this.

We can teach people to make commitments, to overcome fear, to deal transparently, to initiate, and to plan a course.

We can teach people to desire lifelong learning, to express themselves, and to innovate.

And just as important, it's vital that we acknowledge that we can *unteach* bravery and creativity and initiative. And that we have been doing just that.

School has become an industrialized system, working on a huge scale, that has significant by-products, including the destruction of many of the attitudes and emotions we'd like to build our culture around.

In order to efficiently jam as much testable data into each generation of kids, we push to make those children compliant, competitive zombies.

What Is Art?

Conceptual art is a new idea, about fifty years old. Of course, at their heart, all plays and poems and organizations are nothing but conceptual art. The concept is the point, not just the craft.

Conceptual art, though, moves far beyond paintbrushes or chisels or what we used to consider talent. Painting has become a tiny sideshow now that the future of the entire economy is an art project. By separating craft from art, we gain a deeper understanding of what art means to us; at the same time we make it clear that those without fine motor skills can still choose to be artists.

When Beckett first published the conceptual play *Waiting for Godot*, he confused a lot of people. A play where nothing much happens, taking place on a set that was apparently pieced together in an afternoon. This is a play?

Sol LeWitt has art on the walls of galleries around the world, but it's probably not painted by him. Instead, Sol invented rules, algorithms, and instructions, and the craft of painting his work directly on the wall is handled by an uncredited painter. To spend time looking at the work of Sol LeWitt is to understand his art, not to admire his brushwork.

John Cage made a ruckus with his silent work, 4'33", which caused confusion and disdain, but again, few would argue that Cage is not an artist.

Art, it seems, is something that is made by an artist.

And an artist is someone who does something for the first time, something human, something that touches another. As Lewis Hyde explained in *The Gift*, it's the connection of spirit and dreams that turns the work of one person into art. You receive Picasso's gift every time you see one of his paintings—this idea, this emotion, it's yours, here, take it.

It's not art if the world (or at least a tiny portion of it) isn't transformed in some way. And it's not art if it's not generous. And most of all, it's not art if there's no risk.

The risk isn't the risk of financial ruin (though that might be part of it). No, the risk is the risk of rejection. Of puzzlement. Of stasis.

Art requires the artist to care, and to care enough to do something when he knows that it might not work.

Today, in the face of the greatest revolution of our time, we are all artists. Or at least we all have the opportunity to be artists. The only thing holding us back is us.

Aren't you tired of pretending you can't make a difference?

The Pieces of Art

Art is personal.

Art is untested.

Art is intended to connect.

Personal because it must reflect the artist. Something the artist believes or wants to say or do or change.

Untested because art is original. The second time is a performance at best.

And *intended to connect* because art unshared is invulnerable, selfish, and ultimately pointless. If your work can't fail because it was never designed to connect, then I respectfully say that you might have had fun creating something beautiful, but it's not art. Just as you can't have heads without tails, you can't have the bright light of artistic success without the scary risk of failing to connect.

Art Is Now Part of the Productive World

One ghetto that we used to reserve for artists was the idea that they made luxury items, entertainments and objects that had nothing to do with productivity or utility.

I think that was convenient but wrong, even fifty years ago.

Thomas Edison was a monopolist (and an artist). Henry Ford's slavish devotion to his concept of interchangeable parts and mass production was as much an art project as an opportunity to make money. Madame Curie gave her life to doing the art of real science. And it's impossible to listen to Martin Luther King Jr. give a speech without acknowledging the very real art (and passion) he brought to his tribe.

Venture capitalists never choose company founders who are merely replacing their day jobs. They seek the CEO who is engaged at a human level, who has chosen this journey because it is the best (and possibly only) way for her to speak up and lead and connect. So yes, it's an art project, and she's an artist. (The local Subway sandwich shop, on the other hand, is boring on purpose.)

While the soloists and the founders get the press, we find the same behaviors in short supply (and highly sought after) in companies and nonprofits as well. Consider the nurse who transforms the floor of the hospital where she works or the mechanic who puts in the extra effort that brings customers back again and again. No, not every organization gets it. Most are still stuck measuring the wrong things.

In a previous book, I called the person we can't live without a linchpin. The linchpin is the cornerstone of a project, the responsibility taker, the one we would miss if she were gone.

The artist is almost certainly a linchpin, but I'm adding another dimension here—it turns out that expending emotional labor, working without a map, and driving in the dark involve confronting fear and living with the pain of vulnerability. The artist comes to a détente with these emotions and, instead of fighting with them, dances with them.

The linchpin connects as a result of the indispensable nature of her contribution. The artist, on the other hand, connects because that's what art is. The artist touches part of what it means to be truly human and does that work again and again.

The invitation to make art is precious. To ignore it is to invite despair.

The Pain of Emotional Labor

Few would argue with the idea that hard work with a pickax or a shovel or a scalpel is to be rewarded. It's grueling and risky and difficult.

Emotional labor is the labor that's in demand today. Not the grueling work of toiling in the sun but the frightening work of facing our shadows. Why be vulnerable if it hurts so much?

If the goal is to make an impact and to be valued for our contribution, the opportunity is to embrace those laborious tasks that are so easy to avoid. While it makes sense to seek shortcuts to improve our productivity, the emotional labor that needs to be done offers no shortcuts. While it's human nature to ask for a guarantee that our labor will be rewarded, the emotional labor that needs to be done offers no guarantees. Which is precisely why it's labor.

You go to work to do your work, and your work is to confront the things that scare you.

The Joy of Emotional Labor

We've been seduced. Seduced into avoiding (and fearing) the fear of art.

We accept the grinding banality of sameness, of compliance, of sitting still in a cubicle or swallowing our pride in a meeting. We call this work, and we've been told to suck it up, because it's our job.

But when the fear of art shows up, suddenly we panic and flee.

What happens when we embrace the fear instead? What happens when we realize that doing emotional labor is just as human as (if not more so than) the physical labor we accept as part of the deal?

To do this very different sort of hard work is thrilling. It's the opportunity to do what only humans can do, and to do it differently every time.

This is who you are meant to be. An artist. Doing the incredibly difficult work of connection.

The Typo Trap

Let me show you how pervasive the industrial mind-set is.

If I show you a political tract or a blog post or a remarkable new poduct with text that contains a typo, what's your first reaction?

If all you can do is say, "You're missing an *r* in the second paragraph," you've abandoned your humanity in favor of becoming a spell checker.

Compliance over inspiration.

Sure, yes, please, let's kill all the typos. But first, let's make a difference.

Correct is fine, but it is better to be interesting.

The Invisible Line in the Sand

Of course, it's not in the sand, it's in our minds. One side of the line says, "I'm an artist, I'm okay with the pain, I commit to the strategy, I will make a ruckus." The other side says, "Hide me."

I believe the line is an essential tool—it grounds us and gives us the leverage to figure out where to go next (and helps us get there). If your bias is to hide, then making art will always feel like an elusive goal, a temporary detour. On the other hand, once you've crossed over and agreed to live this life, then the only way to deal with art is to make more art.

Does thinking about the line make you uncomfortable? I hope so. That's the first step in crossing it.

I Couldn't Do That

My friend Joss has a stellar résumé. She's had high-level jobs in marketing at some pretty well-known companies. And now, like many people, she's looking for a new gig, a job that will help her use her skills to make a difference. And now, like many people, she's getting frustrated at how difficult it's turning out to be to replicate the last job she had.

We brainstormed for a few hours and I shared some approaches she could use to jump-start her search, to earn the trust and respect of people in the industry who might want to hire her. She said, "That's way outside my comfort zone."

The invisible line, right in front of the two of us. She had said something so true, something so relevant, that I actually gasped.

I explained that she had already explored all the things that were *inside* her comfort zone, and in a competitive market she was going to have to stretch the boundaries of how she would engage the marketplace. She didn't ask the economy to change, but it did.

It's what we wrestle with every single day. The intersection of comfort, danger, and safety. The balancing act between vulnerability and shame. The opportunity (or the risk) to do art. The willingness to take responsibility for caring enough to make a difference and to have a point of view.

Moving your comfort zone when the safety zone changes isn't easy, but it's better than being a victim.

Connection Causes Change

Everyone you interact with is changed forever.

The only questions are:

How will they be different? and

How different will they be?

Author Michael Schrage wants you to ask, "Who do you want your customers to become?"

At first this seems like a ridiculous question. Your customers are your customers. Your coworkers are your coworkers.

This isn't true. Connection creates change. Unless you are selling a standard commodity, the interactions you have with the market change the market. Zappos turned its customers into people who demand a higher level of service to be satisfied. Amazon turned its customers into people who are restless with online stores that don't work quite as well or quite as quickly. Henry Ford turned his customers from walkers into drivers.

When you disappoint someone (or exceed their expectations), that interaction is going to color all the interactions that person has tomorrow and next year.

Apple is talked about more than any other company for one simple reason: They have huge aspirations for who they want their customers to become, and they deliver on them.

Who will your customers become after they interact with you?

Who will you become as a result?

The industrialist doesn't think a lot about interactions or change. He focuses on filling today's need at the highest yield. The artist, though, is obsessed with connection and thus change. You are not the same person you were a year ago. Are you more cynical? More skilled? Who have you become?

There are countless paths available to each of us, and more still available to those whom we'd seek to serve. Answering Schrage's question honestly gives you a chance to describe the change you want to see in the world. Not at the Henry Ford industrial-scale level, of course. No, but even if you connect with six people, you are changing them.

Changing them how? Whom do you want them to become?

I'd like you to become an artist. To make connections that matter. That's my mission.

Connection Doesn't Play the Short Game

Do not expect applause. Accept applause, sure, please do.

But when you *expect* applause, when you do your work in order to get (and because of) applause, you have sold yourself short. When your work depends on something out of your control, you have given away part of your art. If your work is filled with the hope and longing for applause, it's no longer your work—the dependence on approval in this moment has corrupted it, turned it into a process in which you are striving for ever more approval.

This is tricky, so bear with me.

There's a huge difference between the shallow pleasure of instant applause and the long-lasting impact of true connection. It's easy to market and manipulate your way into the quick smile or the Broadway-theater obligatory standing ovation.

What's more difficult is to do the less-congratulated work of getting under someone's skin, of changing the conversation, and of being missed when you're gone.

Who decides if your work is good? When you are at your best, *you* do. If the work doesn't deliver on its purpose, if the pot you made leaks or the hammer you forged breaks, then you should learn to make a better one. The purpose of your art is to connect, just as the purpose of the hammer is to strike the nail.

But we don't blame the nail for breaking the hammer or blame the water for leaking from the pot. If the audience doesn't like this work enough to connect, there's a mismatch. Perhaps this is the wrong work for the wrong group. Don't fix it by pandering for a quick ovation. Fix it by going deeper.

"Here, here it is; it's finished."

If it's finished, the applause, the thanks, the gratitude are something else. Something extra and not part of what you created. If you play a beautiful song for two people or a thousand, it's the same song, and the amount of thanks you receive isn't part of that song.

The connection that comes after the art is appreciated lasts far longer than applause ever could and opens the door for you to work to create ever more connection, as opposed to seeking to repeat the evanescent thrill of an ovation.

Everyone is lonely. Connect.

PART TWO

Myths, Propaganda, and *Kamiwaza*

Myths and dreams come from the same place. . . .
A myth is the society's dream.

—Joseph Campbell

Just a Myth

Where do our myths come from? Do they mean anything?

Why do we continue to talk about Hercules, Thor, and Ronald Reagan? Why are stories of Zeus, Moses, and Martin Luther King Jr. so resonant?

When we bring up the Mahatma or Steve Jobs, are we talking about real people or the ideas behind them?

Joseph Campbell (himself a mythological figure) nailed it. Myths aren't about gods (real ones or imagined). *They are about us.* They are about humans acting human but doing it while wearing the cloaks of gods, of legendary figures. Myths highlight the very best of ourselves (and sometimes the worst). These stories don't spread because a king or despot insists that we hear them and memorize them. No, we engage with and remember and resonate with myths because they're about our favorite person, our best possible self.

Myths aren't myths at all. They are mirrors, paths to walk, and bars to be exceeded. The forgotten part of the original story of Icarus was a powerful talisman, a reminder to avoid selling ourselves short, a reminder to honor the opportunities in front of us.

The Cottage, the Castle, and the Cathedral

Campbell explains that the ancient myths and folktales came from three places. From the cottage we got folk stories for the entertainment of kids—Paul Bunyan and David Curhan. Timeless myths came from the castle (government, royalty, defense) and the cathedral (organized religions). These myths were designed to elevate, to encourage patriotism and obedience and, yes, heroism.

Ancient myths revolve around ancient sources of power. They celebrate kings and generals, priests and chieftains.

Our parents' myths, though, came from a very different place. For them it was the threat of annihilation coming from the Kremlin, the bright promise of college, and the legendary power of the corporation that created the stories we were told. These new sources of power (and risk) led to a very different set of modern myths. We told stories of a different sort of industrial outcome, myths about fitting in and obedience and not getting too uppity.

And these myths resonated with our parents (and with us) because they made us feel like there was a path available for us to take. They resonated because society reflected the modern myths at the same time that it enforced them. The myths of the company man and the college boy and the jock and the happy homemaker were swallowed whole. We saw in them the dreams society had for us, and we made those dreams our dreams.

In fact, they were our faith. We believed in the promise and accepted the offer of the industrialist. "We will do this if you will give us that." This is why Betty Friedan and George Carlin were such a threat. They had the guts to challenge the modern faith of the industrial regime.

Within a generation, the Homeric myths of bravery and guts were supplanted by the workaday unbrave myths of *Leave It to Beaver* and Archie Bunker. Sure, there were still superheroes in the comic books hidden under our beds, but these heroes were never meant to be us—they were the idle pastimes of boys who hadn't yet come to realize that the army had no room for Captain America and that, yes, in fact, Spider-Man couldn't get a job. Our parents bought us Batman Underoos and Superman T-shirts, but it was clearly stated: You can pretend to be a hero, but you are not one, and you will grow up to be an obedient member of society.

Myths can be subtle and insidious. We integrate them into our culture and repeat them until they not only sound true but are true. These modern myths grew side by side with the power of the industrial economy, and they exist to serve the purposes of those who rule our economy and our systems.

Hubris is the enemy of this ruling class. Hubris means that you have the voice to challenge authority and the guts to stand up and speak out. It's not surprising, then, that the only part of the Icarus story we're left with is the warning about hubris.

The hubris of art, though, is precisely what we need right now.

Propaganda Is Not Myth

Propaganda at its best is mythlike. Soviet posters urging hard work, Nazi films celebrating national unity. Corporate training films that soft-pedal but insist on compliance in the name of diversity. Modern, corporate stories are increasingly part of our lives, and the creators of these stories would like you to believe that they are just like myths—resonant stories about our true selves.

It's the opposite. These aren't myths at all. *Propaganda is a set of stories about what someone in power would like you to be.* What they're insisting you become. Propaganda in the industrial age has created generations who believe that consistent obedience to the powerful is part of who we are. One definition of propaganda: It benefits the teller, not the recipient.

Propaganda urges us to become someone we aren't. And it works if the creator of the propaganda has the rewards or the power to make it stick.

Myths are about becoming more godlike and achieving our best. Propaganda, on the other hand, celebrates those in power and urges us to willingly comply with their desires.

The Banality of Our Propaganda

In 1757, on behalf of the British East India Company, a small British force took over part of India, installing a puppet governor. Over the nearly two hundred years that followed, India came under increasingly tight control by commercial and colonial interests.

How do you do that? How do you subjugate an entire country, one of the largest on earth, with only a tiny army at your disposal?

At many points, the British were outnumbered on the ground by more than a million to one.

The answer was to create a set of stories and expectations that changed the culture. Indian culture was manipulated, with a new ruling class inserted atop a millennium-old tradition of stratification. The English dominated India because they sold the Indians propaganda, not because they had better guns.

Propaganda was turned into mythlike stories and expectations. Subservience and placid acceptance of control were sold as virtues, and sold consistently. If what you dream of when you dream of success matches what the overlords need from you, stability follows.

This goes far beyond India and imperial power. Popular culture as we understand it has been around since colonial times. It is informed by the economics that got us here in the first place. As a result, we have touchstones based on mercantilism, imperialism, and capitalism. The things that made us wealthy enough to have a pop culture also determined the way we see the world.

Our factory-driven culture has worked overtime to sell us this propaganda:

Don't make trouble.
Follow the leader.
Fit in even when it hurts.
Teamwork is what we call it when you do what the boss says.
Settle down.
Teach your children to obey.
The tall poppy gets cut down; the tallest nail gets hammered.
Trust the system to take care of you.
Don't fly too close to the sun.

This propaganda gets under your skin. It seeps in and changes you. How does this quote from Caterina Fake, founder of Flickr, make you feel?

What is more pleasant than the benevolent notice other people take of us, what is more agreeable than their compassionate empathy? What inspires us more than addressing ears flushed with excitement, what captivates us more than exercising our own power of fascination? What is more thrilling than an entire hall of expectant eyes, what more overwhelming than applause surging up to us? What, lastly, equals the enchantment sparked off by the delighted attention we receive from those who profoundly delight ourselves?—*Attention by other people is the most irresistible of drugs.* To receive it outshines receiving any other kind of income. This is why glory surpasses power and why wealth is overshadowed by prominence [emphasis added].

Can you even imagine a boss or a teacher or a colonial overlord eagerly selling this idea to an underling? What about the tall poppies? What about fear of failure, the fear of critics, and the Icarus Deception—failing to remind us not to fly too low? Caterina Fake is spouting heresy.

Individual achievement and the insanity of art fly in the face of what our corporate culture seeks out. Whether the art is done for the glory or for the innate satisfaction it generates, art threatens those who would prefer to sell us a fear of hubris instead.

We've been sold, and sold hard, on the appeal of the banality of factory work, and not just in our day jobs. While we occasionally celebrate the outliers, the mythological gods of our culture, it is always with the understanding that *they are not us*. You can be a fan of Prince, Leonard Bernstein, or Lady Gaga, but the rule is that you must understand that you have no chance of becoming them. They are gods of myth and you are merely a consumer.

You have no idea what you're doing. If you did, you'd be an expert, not an artist.

A Little Bucket of Fear and a Backpack Full of Loneliness

The fear has been shifted. It went from the wild animal's fear for survival, the fear of the dark and of predators, to the industrialist-invented fear of noncompliance, fear of authority, fear of standing out.

The industrialist offers us a trade. We can trade in our loneliness for the embrace of the mob and trade our innate fears for a steady paycheck. We can trade our yearning for something great in exchange for the safety of knowing that we will be taken care of. In return, all he asks is that we give up our humanity.

When you look at it clearly, it's hardly a fair trade. Better, I think, to choose art, with all that it brings.

Trapped

The ladder of success isn't a ladder. It's a series of steps with leaps interspersed along the way.

Those lucky enough to start with a supportive mentor and access to resources begin walking up the ladder and, with some pluck, can move quite high in the industrial pecking order.

But then they come to that spot where following instructions is no longer sufficient—where they're required to give instructions instead. They'll hit a gap where the only way to get across is to make rules instead of following them. And like most people indoctrinated by the industrial system, they'll freeze, trapped between where they are and where they want to be.

The Popular One Wears a Mask

Seeking to become popular is not hardwired into human nature. What all of us seek is positive reinforcement, and our culture reinforces behaviors that we believe will make us popular.

Is there any doubt that it's fun and safe and reassuring to be the popular kid? Certainly at first, at least in our culture, the rush of pleasure and security that comes from the positive feedback of popularity is intoxicating.

But pity the cute kid who gets anointed as the popular one or the class clown who discovers that a rude joke works or the facile actor who succeeds early and often in school plays. The feedback that comes from popularity in a popularity-obsessed system becomes an addiction.

Soon the cuteness fades or the jokes get old or other, harder-working actors and musicians take the stage. Now what? How does the popular one stay popular?

The cycle begins. Instead of artistry, she buys into the cycle of short-term pleasing. Instead of standing up for things he believes in, he calculates what the audience wants to hear right now.

And this cycle prepares us brilliantly for a life as a corporate cog, a tool for the industrial system. When Willy Loman talked about being well liked, he was embracing the propaganda of the mask. "The man who makes an appearance in the business world, the man who creates personal interest, is the man who gets ahead. Be liked and you will never want."

In order to be liked, though, you might have to trade in your true, vulnerable self for a short term–focused obsession with pleasing the masses.

What Loman learned, and what so many of us are learning, is that in fact the system will gladly eat your orange and then throw the peel away.

The goal needs to shift. The opportunity is not in being momentarily popular with the anonymous masses. It's in being missed when you're gone, in doing work that matters to the tribe you choose.

The old system made you popular for fitting in. The new one gives you a chance to stand out.

Prideful and Disobedient

Countless myths involve punishing a god (Loki, Satan, Theseus) for the sins of pride and disobedience.

Theseus, the great king, the powerful general, the revered leader, spent years chained to a rock, tortured for having the temerity to visit the underworld. He grasped too far.

It's easy to see why those in power, those running the castle or the cathedral (or even the cottage), would want to spread the word about these disloyal behaviors, to warn us off from imagining that we could walk as the gods walk.

Art, though, requires both pride *and* disobedience. The pride of creation and the disobedience of disturbing the status quo.

Operant Conditioning

B. F. Skinner taught us that cues that lead to rewards create habits. If you're rewarded when you do something, you're likely to do it again. If that happens enough, it becomes a habit.

Where does the habit of compliance come from?

Could it be the alarm clock and the penalty for coming in late that create the habit of going to work every morning? Perhaps the habit of shopping for fun comes from the ten thousand advertising messages you see every day, most of which are about either fitting in or spending the money you earned by fitting in. It could be that the habit of being part of the system comes from the stultifying meetings and the relentless pressure to go to a famous college and get a job.

Virtually every moment in industrial society presents another chance to be conditioned to do factory work, instead of challenging the status quo and making art that's never been made before. All the immediate rewards go to those who increase productivity right now.

If you want to find yourself making art, set up some new habits. Abandon the habit of avoiding negative notes in your e-mail ("Phew, everything's still okay"), and replace it with the habit of measuring how many frontiers you crossed today.

Six Daily Habits for Artists

Sit alone; sit quietly.

Learn something new without any apparent practical benefit.

Ask individuals for bold feedback; ignore what you hear from the crowd.

Spend time encouraging other artists.

Teach, with the intent of making change.

Ship something that you created.

The Impresario Opportunity

An impresario? Yes, someone who organizes, who invents, who creates art projects, who spins something out of nothing, using insight and connection more than money.

If you owned a conference facility, what would you do with it? Of course, you *could* own it, at least a day at a time.

If you could reach your audience, what would you say? Of course you can reach them, more easily and more effectively than ever before (not faster, though, but over time).

If you could lead a tribe (customers, coworkers, fellow scientists), which tribe would you lead?

The ability to create connections, establish events, and make something happen is more highly leveraged, faster, and cheaper than ever before.

Your job isn't to do your job. Your job is to decide what to do next.

The Impresario and the Entrepreneur

In the industrial economy we had a name for the rogue, for the individual who bucked the top-down system of power. We called him an entrepreneur. A brave soul might solicit money and time, and in exchange his investors would expect him to build something bigger than himself, a venture that had a chance to enter the ranks of the industrial mighty.

Edison and Case and Bezos were entrepreneurs, tirelessly taking corporate risks to build significant ventures.

But impresarios don't have to follow only this path.

The impresario puts on a show, weaving together nothing and ending up with everything.

The first impresarios put on opera performances. They found the talent, booked the theater, hung signs, and sold tickets. No impresario, no music.

The impresario is a pathfinder. She's the person who figures out what to do next—and then does it. She improvises.

She figures out how to use the connections enabled by the connection economy to create value where none existed before, and how to transform a "no" into a "yes."

The junior partner who takes initiative to start a weekly conference series or the cello player who organizes an annual music festival—these are impresarios without a business plan or a board of directors. When someone cares enough to connect and lead and initiate, it doesn't matter where she works or what her job title is; she's doing an art project and flying higher than the rest of us.

The impresarios of our time don't always sell tickets and they don't always work on their own. They might be the person down the hall who organized the off-site meeting when none was planned. Or the business-development person who reached out to precisely the right partner at precisely the right time.

The cog waits for instructions. The entrepreneur often needs an exit in sight. But the impresario takes what's available and makes magic.

It's not necessarily about the money or even a business, and it's certainly not about building an industrial empire. It might merely be about the joy of doing art.

No, we're not all entrepreneurs, not at all. But we are all able to be artists, and all artists are impresarios.

Worldviews Run Deep

The way you view the world wasn't set on the day you were born, but it has no doubt gelled by now. The culture we grow up in and the rewards we receive for the actions we take combine to give every person a set of biases and shortcuts in how information is processed and decisions are made.

Our worldview changes the questions we ask ourselves when confronted by a new situation or idea. The questions you ask yourself change the way you perceive the world.

I'm arguing that there's an inherent worldview difference here. There are industrialists, who see the world as broken or fixed, and artists, who see the world as a series of projects to be built and connections to be made. Whether the projects work isn't as important as how they're built. Industrialists like things to be functional, and they admire competence, so the idea of breaking things on purpose by pursuing the new is threatening indeed.

The industrialist asks, "How does this threaten me?" or perhaps "How can I use this to make gradual improvements in the systems I have?" Most of all, he asks, "Is it safe?"

The artist wonders, "How can I break this?" or "Where is there an opportunity for me to change everything and make an impact?" Most of all, the question is "Is it interesting?"

Author Cassidy Dale points out that many people are either

knights or gardeners. The knights view the world as a cataclysmic conflict with winners and losers, with battles to be fought, and with right and wrong as the dominant drivers. Gardeners, on the other hand, have the instinct to look for ways to heal, to connect, and to grow the people they encounter. These biases affect the way people buy groceries, practice a religion (or not), and vote.

Arnold Toynbee chronicled the dominant worldviews in dozens of civilizations over thousands of years and divided them into cultures that saw winners and losers and cultures that focused on responses to challenges instead.

In each generalization, no one is rigid, a perfect example, always seeing the world precisely as described. But it's also true that these worldviews run deep, and they change the way we interpret events in the world, the people in it, and even this book.

If you're not seeing the world through the eyes of an artist, you'll never truly embrace the revolution that's going on around you. The opportunity (and the challenge) is to temporarily suspend disbelief, put on the artist's hat (beret?), and imagine what happens when you see the world of connection as an opportunity, as opposed to a problem to be solved.

A Few Worldview Questions to Consider:

How do I get more? vs. How do I give more?

How do I guarantee success? vs. How do I risk failure?

Where is the map? vs. Where is the wilderness?

Do I have enough money? vs. Have I made enough art?

Where Are the Gods?

The old work: Bale that cotton, mow that hay, load that barge. Fill in this form, obey these instructions, take this test.

The new work: Start something. Figure it out. Connect. Make the call. Ask. Learn. Repeat. Risk it. Open. What's next?

The old work is machinelike.

The new work is for mythological gods.

Gods in charge of their destiny. Gods responsible for their choices. Gods with power and the freedom to use it.

Us.

Helen Keller Is a Myth

Of course she lived and inspired us. But now, like Miles Davis and Galileo and John Brown, she is a mythical figure, more an inspiring story than a real person.

Twenty-five hundred years ago, Euhemerus argued that all the myths are inspired by the lives of humans, by kings and holy men. He pinpointed the grave of Zeus and told us that the stories we told one another were here to inspire us to become greater than ourselves.

The purpose of myths is not to have us feel separate from the gods in the stories but to have us understand that we are capable of the great feats that they perform.

Myths Are Ancient Truths About What We Are Capable Of

Our gods are so human.

The deities we create are a lot like us, at our best. Hercules, the son of Zeus, is an idealized man. He looks as though he might appear on the cover of *Men's Fitness*, and he displays the valor of a decorated member of the Special Forces. Whether or not Hercules ever walked the earth, there is a bit of him inside of us.

Consider Omoikane, a Japanese god of wisdom and insight, a deity capable of making decisions that we would make if we only had the time. On a good day we share some of his knowledge, some of his ability to see the world as it is.

Superman, Thor, Moses, Athena, George Gershwin, Thomas Edison—they each represent part of what it is to be human; they are inside all of us. We know we are capable of this—to be that strong or that cool or that generous. To persevere and connect and contribute the way our gods can—that's why we invented them, why we revere them, and why they resonate with us. We have them inside, every day.

And yet we have no perfect word for expressing godlike abilities. We don't know how to talk about what it is to perform in a mythological way, to strip away the artifice and let the deity express itself.

And the Icarus Deception pushes us to avoid even thinking of it. It strikes deep into our psyche with a vivid warning about the dangers of hubris.

Too late.

We've built a world where the only option *is* hubris, where the future belongs to anyone willing to act like the gods of our myths. Better coin a word for it.

The Japanese call it *kamiwaza*.

Kamiwaza Requires Us to Embrace Our Humanity

If the gods are us, then do we dare be as the gods are?

The Japanese term *kamiwaza*, like most great words for which we have no equivalent, is difficult to translate. The shortest version is "godlike."

When we strip away self-doubt and artifice, when we embrace initiative and art, we are left with *kamiwaza*. The purity of doing it properly but without self-consciousness. The runner who competes with *kamiwaza* is running with purity, running properly, running as the gods would run.

How dare we! How dare we presume to ignore Daedalus, to fly close to the sun, to apparently forgo humility in a quest for something unattainable?

How can we *not* dare?

Hubris makes us godlike, and being godlike makes us human.

Please, Let's Not Talk About Humility Yet

We have plenty of humility. We've built layers of propaganda to reinforce the false humility of the worker who settles for less and for the student who doesn't ask difficult questions and for the artist who hides her art out of fear of offending someone.

Even Orwell was embarrassed by the egoism in his writing: "The great mass of human beings are not acutely selfish. After the age of about thirty they abandon individual ambition—in many cases, indeed, they almost abandon the sense of being individuals at all—and live chiefly for others, or are simply smothered under drudgery. But there is also the minority of gifted, wilful people who are determined to live their own lives." I don't think Orwell was selfish. I think Orwell had something to say, and I'm glad he said it.

Yes, there is a lesson to be learned from the hubris of Icarus, from his impatient desire to fly high without understanding the implications of his actions. But no, we don't have a humility shortage, we don't have too many citizens actively sharing their best and most generous ideas, we don't have too many caring leaders eagerly building up dignity among their followers.

We are consumed with the humility of asking for directions, following the leader, and playing it safe. We have embraced the humility of not taking initiative and of designing a life where we can't possibly be blamed.

Until we have a humility shortage, then, the real problem is this: We continue to fly too low. We're so afraid of demonstrating hubris, so afraid of the shame of being told we flew too high, so paralyzed by the fear that we won't fit in, that we buy into the propaganda and don't do what we are capable of.

Art Requires a Commitment to *Kamiwaza*

All the rewards for creating art are not present at its creation. That's because the art isn't truly art until it has connected you with another, until it has made contact and touched someone else. You take your art and move it from here to there with nothing but daring and faith and passion, and only after you land do you discover if your art was deemed "good."

This is the huge difference between art and direct marketing, between art and doing your job, between art and just about everything else we do in life. In all the other parts of our lives, the deal is "If you do this, you *will* get that." In the world of art, the deal is "Well, other people have done something sort of like what you're hoping to do, and sometimes, but certainly not always, it works out for them. You'll have to do it to find out."

The hubris involved in this decision is extraordinary. "Maybe this will work," we wonder. Or even, for the particularly committed, "This might not work." We've been taught that only a mythological god has the right to approach the world with that sort of confidence—confidence that no matter what happens, the journey itself was worth it.

Unfortunately for those considering a timid step into the world of art, the odds of external success start small and grow slowly. So we can't just commit to one act of *kamiwaza*, one bold emotional risk, and be done with it. We have to commit to a lifetime of them. It's a process, not an event. You don't do a little art and then go back to work. Your work is your art (and vice versa).

Of course, art isn't done only for the external rewards, though sometimes the external rewards permit us to keep making art.

When a work of art fails, don't question your commitment to art. You can question how you see, how you make, how good (in quotes) your art was, but the artist in you won't waste time questioning the commitment to art.

When your art fails, *make better art.*

Better Art, Three Ways

Fly closer to the sun.

Become naked and vulnerable in front of those you give your art to, and

Seek to make a connection.

The question isn't whether you are capable
of godlike work. (You are.)

The question is: Are you willing?

Confusing the Venue (or the Medium)
with Our Art

A paintbrush or a spatula isn't your art. Neither is a particular
building or a programming language.

You don't commit to a venue or a medium or a technique. You
commit to a path and an impact. Broadway is a venue. Joy through
movement is an art. When the venue doesn't support your art, you
can change it without changing your commitment to the journey.

The waitress who is an artist doesn't work for tips. She does her
work, bringing enthusiasm and making connections, because this
is her passion. If her clientele doesn't respond in this particular
restaurant, there's no humiliation in putting on that show in a different one. Or in moving her venue from a restaurant to a nightclub
or a classroom.

Enjoying the Journey

One of the disconnects of our language is the confusion between
enjoying a vacation, the somnambulistic, disconnected, drunken
haze of lying on the beach, and enjoying your art, the sometimes
frightening, grueling, high-stakes work of making a difference.

No one wonders why successful musicians keep touring or successful authors keep writing even after they have no need to make

a living. We don't wonder because we understand and envy the joy that comes from performing what you love, the satisfaction that comes from making art instead of following instructions.

The joy of art is particularly sweet, though, because it carries with it the threat of rejection, of failure, and of missed connections. It's precisely the high-wire act of "this might not work" that makes original art worth doing. (Which is one reason you would have had trouble hearing Van Morrison perform "Moondance" live in concert—he wanted to make a ruckus, not be a jukebox).

It's probably enjoyable to trade in your initiative and heart to take a job where you are told precisely what to do. It feels like a safe bet, but it actually means you've accepted a low-grade, throbbing ennui in exchange for the thrill of daring the gods. Many of us were deceived enough by industrial propaganda to buy into the promise of this kind of sleepwalking.

The artists you know, though, want none of that. They'd rather take a different path, intentionally seeking out opportunities to connect, to succeed, and to fail. They'd rather be awake.

You can pretend to enjoy the industrial substitute for a life well lived, but if you experience your humanity without the craft you were indoctrinated in, you might discover a different sort of journey.

When We Hesitate to Commit, We Sabotage the Art

On January 1, 2012, I ripped my hamstring pretty badly. More than six months later, I still don't run or even walk with *kamiwaza*. Not because it hurts or because I have seriously limited range of motion (I'm lucky enough to have neither problem). No, it's because I can't leap. I can't leap because part of my brain hesitates. Not for long, but just enough to move my entire body off kilter.

This confidence, the fearlessness of forward motion without attachment to what will happen on the landing, is the signal we send to ourselves and to the world when we're ready to do something artful. Giving up our attachment to what might happen—maybe the boss won't like it, maybe the market will reject it, maybe my friends will think it's stupid—is an essential part of commitment.

We make the art and *then* we get the feedback, but the art must happen first. If we're in love with the feedback and trying to manipulate the applause we get, we'll cease to make the art we're capable of.

When the critic pushes you to make better art, art that you are capable of, then her response is worth cherishing. But the critic who pushes you to fit in or dumb down your work—take that criticism with caution.

Attachment Kills Art

It's easy to become attached to potential outcomes. We want the cake to come out just so, or the audience to clap at this particular spot, or every single person on Yelp to like our pizza.

As we become attached to these positive outcomes, we start to imagine what will happen if they don't occur. So we alter what we make to increase the chances that they will occur. And when they don't (and the things we get attached to never happen every time), we start to question our art and to alter it even more.

And then we're no longer making art. We're a marionette controlled by those in power.

What is needed, rather than running away or
controlling or suppressing or any other resistance,
is understanding fear; that means, watch it,
learn about it, come directly into contact with it.
We are to learn about fear, not how to escape
from it.

—Jiddu Krishnamurti

Art and Love

I don't love you because of what you do. I love you. I'm committed.
Now that this is settled, what are you going to do?

Love is a commitment to a person, not to that person's behavior.

This commitment to the bumpy journey is stressful for people
raised in an industrial economy, where everything appears to be for
sale, where grades and feedback and sales and raises and job security and Twitter followers are driven by the quid pro quo of "*do this/
get that.*" But if you're going to be loved anyway, your behavior
doesn't have to be driven by your yearning for an outcome; it can
be driven by something deeper.

And this prospect is frightening, because it means you can't
measure the outcome while you're planning and executing your
art, and it requires you to commit to your actions, separate from
any attachment you might have to what might happen next.

Art is a commitment to a process and to a direction and to
generosity, not to a result.

When we make art without attachment, we're approaching *kamiwaza*.

Critics Are Always Wrong About "Everyone" . . .

. . . but they're entitled to their opinions.

The worst sort of critic relies on a time-honored crutch, one that rarely works: "I didn't like it; therefore no one will like it."

The critic says, "This play was terrible," when she means, "I didn't like the play, but you might." The critic says, "This book will never sell," when she means, "People who have the same taste as I do won't buy this book."

Universalizing negative feedback takes the pressure off the critic. The critic is putting the blame back on the artist instead of taking responsibility for her opinion.

The one-star reviews on Amazon are an author's bane and a tar pit to be avoided. Of course these people are wrong; they must be corrected! I'm overwhelmed with the desire to point out what they didn't understand in my writing, why they are mistaken. I don't mind errors in taste (there are no errors in taste), but I'm frothing at their errors in judgment! For years I was fixated on these anonymous screeds (the negative ones are just about always anonymous, even in *Publishers Weekly*).

Or worse, the artist starts to believe that the criticism is actually true, that the work is universally lousy, and then the art suffers, because the lizard is activated, the resistance is on high alert, and commitment starts to waver. Gradually, every step carries a small hesitation as the artist becomes attached to the outcome. *Kamiwaza* fades.

The art is too important for these reviews to be indulged. Walk away. Let them be wrong. They are critics. Critics are always wrong.

We're not looking for the correct method, we're looking for the incorrect method.

—Keith Richards

Joe Dough's response to critics

photo by unknown source via *Huffington Post*

Leaping as a Natural Human Instinct

I (at least part of me) was lucky enough to grow up at Camp Arowhon in northern Ontario. Deep in the north woods of Canada, I spent summers confronting what it meant to do what you wanted to do. That was a loaded obligation, because it meant you had to commit and then execute, without being able to blame the predicament of your choice on anyone else.

A highlight of the lake was the twenty-four-foot-high diving board. Looking back, I think the diving board might have been as low as twenty-two feet, but regardless, it was incredibly high. Icarus high.

Painted white, made of almost-rotted wood, and ascended via twenty-one slippery steps, the diving board was a beacon to every kid who saw it. It was dangerous. Awesome in the best sense of the word.

The deal was simple: If you climbed up, you had to jump off. It was too tricky (physically and emotionally) to climb down.

Day after day, new initiates to the cult of the big leap would bravely climb up the tower. Then they'd get to the top and stop. They'd freeze in place, unable to move. Sometimes for hours. One kid once sat there for fourteen hours.

Here's the key question: What happened between the time a kid started climbing the ladder and the internal system failure that occurred at the top of the board? Was there new information presented? When that kid was at the bottom, he was thrilled and excited. At the top, frozen.

Perhaps something changed. At the top, the newbie jumper saw something he hadn't seen from the dock. Nothing visible changed, of course. What changed was the volume of the argument in the leaper's head.

When you're standing on the dock, part of the brain insists on going up. It'll be fun/brave/heroic/daring/wonderful, the adventure-seeking frontal lobe says. The other part, the part that worries about things like belly flops and dying, that part is not sufficiently aroused to stop the jumper from going up the ladder. Later. Later, the lizard brain says, I'll worry about this.

At the top of the tower, though, the dialogue changes dramatically. Death, after all, is apparently imminent. Now the other part of the brain, the one that's often more powerful, speaks up and insists (demands) that this nonsense stop. It's *high*. This is danger-ous. This is insane.

Amazingly, after that first jump, the deflowered leapers always do the same thing.

They get out of the water, run to the steps, climb right back up, and do it again. Safety zone adjusted, comfort zone aligned. For now. And the opportunity is to make it a habit.

The Truth About Roller Coasters

Everyone knows that you're not likely to die on a roller coaster. It's far more dangerous to drive to the amusement park than it is to get on the ride.

And yet. And yet even though we know how safe it is, a good roller coaster terrifies us from the first frightening hill until the relief at the end. That's because it's *designed* to do so. The twists and turns and noise and speed are designed to bypass our rational brain and go straight to the amygdala, our prehistoric brain stem, the part of our brain that's hardwired to avoid danger.

We've built a culture that's filled with virtual roller coasters.

The security theater at the airport is a cultural roller coaster, with the TSA using uniforms and hassle to (they hope) incite fear among some travelers and comfort among the rest. The senior prom is a very different kind of roller coaster, one designed to get a different response, to fill the not-quite-popular kid with just enough shame at the prospect of missing the event that he'll go anyway, because it's safer than not going.

Or consider the job interview, a high-stress situation that would be more effective if it had no stress associated with it—a lion isn't going to eat you, and your fight-or-flight reflex isn't particularly useful here. But that's precisely why some misguided interviewers create the stress—they believe that it shows how you'll perform at work.

The biggest cultural roller coaster of all is the one that pushes us to keep our heads down and comply, the one that is short-circuiting your art. This is the unspoken threat (the one we're reminded of from first grade) that you're just one misstep away from being fired, ostracized, thrown out, and exiled from the community. It's not true, but your lizard brain doesn't know that, any more than it knows that a roller coaster at Six Flags isn't going to kill you.

None of this is rational. All of it is effective, because it touches our fear and shame.

Resilience and the Factory

The profitable factory farm can't handle a radical change in the weather. It's optimized to make money from controlled inputs. The profitable big hotel doesn't easily get transformed into a hospital or a civic center when it's done—it's designed to excel at just one function.

These industries are thoroughbred racehorses, Ferraris capable of going fast if everything is just right.

When the world changes, industrialists get stressed. That's because the industrial system is optimized and polished and stretched to be good at maximizing profit. Like a show dog that could never make it in the wild, industrialism is pampered and brittle.

Artists can't afford to be fragile. The work is a series of projects and problems to be solved, not a pristine, predictable environment where refined inputs lead to ever-more-refined outputs.

Yes, the world is filled with hippos, giant industrial machines that dominate the landscape. Artists are merely the little birds eating their scraps. The thing is, though, that when times change, the resilience and speed and adaptive ability of the artist will easily outlast the lumbering, brittle industrialist.

> I want them to discover that they are artists; everyone is an artist, a creator, and a refiner of sensibility without knowing it.
>
> —Yves Klein

The Talent Myth

When you talk to yourself, who is listening?

We've tried to marginalize the notion of multiple brains. We cruelly ridicule schizophrenics and make fun of the notion of a split personality. But don't we all have one?

One part of us wants to climb the steps, to leap, to fly, to make an impact. The other, the more primitive one, wants to play it safe, to lie low, and to avoid failing.

Our economy has worked overtime to emphasize and reward the lizard. We have built a society around making the artist the exception and heroism the rare instance that proves the rule.

Worst of all, we've invented the notion of the specific talent. The notion that some people are born with godlike abilities for a given endeavor, the talent to paint or speak or write or lead or invent or comfort. The rest of us, the story goes, are drones, the worker bees that are unentitled to the benefits reserved for the few.

And we play along. It doesn't take much for an errant parent, a tired kindergarten teacher, or a short term–focused coach or boss to convince us that in fact there's not much here. Just a few prompts are usually sufficient for us to abandon the art that lies within.

If it's so obvious that some have talent and others don't, why is it so hard to pick the winners and why are we always surprised by the latest unexpected triumph?

Fear of Public Speaking

Of course we're frightened. All the evolutionary cues for danger are present. We have to stand up in front of people—people we might enrage or provoke. We have to speak, perhaps to say something dumb, perhaps to contradict the leader.

We might be banished from the village as a result, left to fend for ourselves among the animals in the jungle.

Of course the lizard brain is on high alert. Of course we'd rather avoid this foolish risk.

Foolish risks are for the gods. That's what we write myths about. Not their everyday, banal lives. No, we write about and talk about and dream about their brave exploits and their foolish risks.

The gods are us. And yes, the gods are crazy.

The Invention of Writer's Block

The term "writer's block" was coined by Edmund Bergler less than a hundred years ago. Here's how the affliction has become an epidemic:

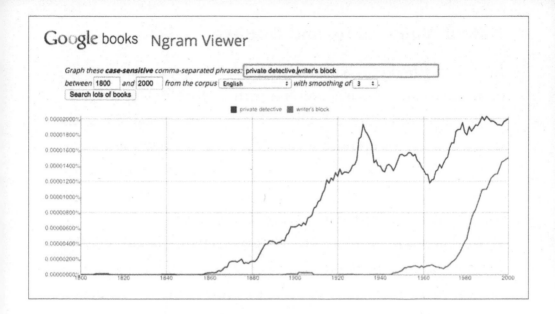

At this rate, there will be more stuck writers than gumshoes in just a few years.

Joan Acocella reports that the resistance took over for writing just as writing became important. A hundred years earlier, it wasn't unusual for writers like Trollope and Dickens to write forty or more books over a career—while keeping a day job. You sat down and you wrote and then you were done.

Starting in the 1950s, though, when writing became godlike, when creating the great American novel had a lot of *kamiwaza* associated with it, the drinking started and so did the blocking. It was easier to talk about making art than it was to actually do it.

And that's where we are today, except that *everything* we're counted on to do that's important is also fraught with risk, because it flies in the face of the easy path of obedience and blame. Everything that matters is like writing, because it's all art.

Naked, Vulnerable, and Godlike

In every myth, there's tension. No god is omnipotent, no action is certain, no one exists in a universe with no pushback or risk.

The gods, when they act, take a risk. They are engaging with the universe, with one another, with the mortal population, and something might happen. And this just might not work out for them.

It's this vulnerability that makes it interesting. And of course, it's the vulnerability that makes each god human.

Author Susan Cain's recent TED talk gets to the heart of this. Cain, author of a book on the power of being an introvert, paradoxically brought the house down by overcoming her shyness in front of a million people. Her story resonates with us not because she's discovered a new truth but because she has, godlike, opened herself up to us, stood up, and announced.

But was she bold? Of course she was. Bold in her vulnerability. Bold in the guts it took to speak quietly, to conquer her fear, to speak up in a whisper when even a whisper felt like a shout. Bold doesn't always mean bellicose or dramatic. It might merely mean connected.

We're drawn to connect with people doing art. They are us at our best. They are the new gods of our myths.

Creating Tension

This is what the powerful public speaker does. It is the work of the photographer or the coach or the teacher who is making a difference.

Tension focuses our attention. Tension brings us closer, eager to find out how the tension will be relieved.

It takes confidence and guts to intentionally create tension.

The workman wants no tension. The cook or the person following instructions in the Dummies guide wants nothing more than to meet spec and avoid the possibility of tension.

But the artist trusts the work and the audience enough to delight in bringing the tension to the boiling point before relieving it.

This Might Not Work

This is a mantra of the artist. And of course, this is where the vulnerability comes from, and the fascination. If you're *sure* it's going to work, where is the tension? "This might work" is the twin sister of "This might not work."

Kamiwaza doesn't mean all-powerful and perfect. If the gods were perfect, there would be no point to the myths we tell. We tell them precisely because the gods aren't perfect—they are merely bold.

The industrialist (your boss, perhaps) demands that everything be proven, efficient, and risk free. The artist seeks none of these. The value of art is in your willingness to stare down the risk and to embrace the void of possible failure.

Change is powerful, but change always comes with the possibility of failure as its partner. "This might not work" isn't merely something to be tolerated; it's something you must seek out.

Sink or Swim

The gods of our myths often face horrible consequences. They are banned from the kingdom or left to be eaten by birds for all eternity.

Our industrial culture doesn't work that way. We talk about "sink or swim," but there's not as much sinking going on as you might expect. There's a fair amount of treading water, a whole lot of people unwilling to get into the pool at all, but not so much sinking.

If a business fails, jobs are lost, lives dislocated; it's true. But no one is burned at the cross; the suffering isn't nearly as long lasting as our fears would have us believe.

Even more encouraging, when an art project fails, it disappears. Punishment isn't meted out; *A*'s are not sewn onto our garments; careers are not dashed for all time.

In fact, in the connection economy, it's the person who doesn't enter the arena who is punished. In the connection economy, the fearful are disconnected. They are the ones who are punished, not by sinking but by being isolated.

We've greatly exaggerated the risk of sinking, without celebrating the value of swimming.

Kamiwaza is actually easier to do than it is to think about.

Once more of us begin to do art, sure, there will be more sinking. But there will be significantly more swimming, more connecting, and more art as well.

There's No Map, but There Is a Choice

Art has no safety map, no easy-to-follow manual, no guaranteed method.

Once those things exist, the art becomes paint by numbers and is hardly worth doing.

Living without a map may make a child of the industrial age uncomfortable. It is life without guarantees, a life where the risks are highly exaggerated and where the banality of life without art is minimized.

Faced with a choice of dying inside as the world mechanizes or confronting the fear that we have been indoctrinated with, many may choose the path of quiet desperation.

Which is your privilege, of course, but understand that it's a choice. The choice between being the linchpin (the one people can't live without) and the cog (who does what she's told). The choice between doing art (and forging your own path, on your own terms, and owning what happens) and merely doing your job (which pushes all the power and all the responsibility to someone else).

The good news is that it's your choice, no one else's.

Welcome, O life, I go to encounter for the millionth time the reality of experience and to forge in the smithy of my soul the uncreated conscience of my race.

—Stephen Dedalus, protagonist in James Joyce's *A Portrait of the Artist as a Young Man*

PART THREE

Grit and Art and the Work That's Worth Doing

True Grit

Grit in a batch of spinach makes it inedible, of course. But worse, far worse, is grit on the assembly line, grit that gets into the finely tuned mechanical pincers or ends up on the bottom of the box or messes with the shiny finish of a Steinway piano.

We're willing to go to great lengths to eliminate it. The army spends billions of dollars to stamp out grit, to find soldiers who won't comply—and to get rid of them. The basic part of basic training is all about eliminating the grit, the burrs and the edges that interfere with the coherence of the group. The army wants the group, not the soldier, to have grit.

All industrial systems abhor grit, the unmeasurable little bits that gum up the works and make outcomes unpredictable. Digital smoothness is the antithesis of grit. Proven processes are the opposite of grit.

Grit is our future.

Our best and brightest future. Perhaps the only hope we've got left.

Grit is the unexpected bump, the decision that cannot be changed, the insistence on a vision, or the ethics of a creator. Grit stands in the way of the short-term compromises of the industrialist.

The grit in your spinach is precisely the same grit that we seek out in a leader or a hero. We measure sandpaper and grindstones in terms of grit—their ability to stand up to resistance. Someone with grit will grind down the opposition, stand up in the face of criticism, and consistently do what's right for their art.

Mostly, they mess up the machine.

Grit Reclaims Our Power

We hesitate to expose our true selves and to speak up and do the work we're capable of because we fear we don't have the power to do so.

And yet some people manage to find that power.

Tenured college professors live in fear of the committee chair or the journal editor or student reviews—except the ones who don't; they stand up and speak up and make an impact.

Assembly-line workers live in fear of the foreman and the union boss—except those who don't; they point out the inefficiencies, the safety issues, and, most important, the overlooked contributors waiting to make a difference.

Creators live in fear of the critic, the sharp-tongued pundit who can take them down with the stroke of a keyboard. Except for those who don't. The ones who don't are willing to take the short-term critical hit and then go on to change our culture.

Grit is the attitude of someone who realizes he has the power to care and is intent on doing something with it.

Relentlessly Removing External Control, Motivation, and Approval

The industrial age—the economy of mass-produced goods and services, the world where efficiency in delivery trumps art—prizes control, leverages external motivation, and uses approval as a weapon to enforce compliance. To make art, you need to remove these three external things:

Control, because external control is the factory. Control means doing what you're told, being part of the machine, a reliable cog. Control abhors grit because it gets in the way of effortless synchronization.

Motivation, because if you rely on external motivation to be your best self, then you will have ceded responsibility and authority to someone else. You will be judged by how well your boss does at motivating you, not based on who you are.

And *approval*, because the crowd is always wrong. The crowd wants bread and circuses; it wants lions and gladiators; it wants *The Beverly Hillbillies* and Justin Bieber. You can do better than the crowd. You can seek your own approval.

Elements of Grit

Psychologist Angela Duckworth and various other authors have outlined elements that combine to give someone that evasive attribute they call grit. Here are the key elements they describe.

PERSEVERANCE: Many people mistake perseverance for grit. Grit includes perseverance, but it comes before the need for perseverance arrives, because grit includes goals and a passion for those goals. Some people will persevere merely because they are instructed to do so. Those with grit will persevere because they believe they have no choice, not if they wish to be who they are.

HARDINESS: The sailor able to survive the long journey, the soldier who doesn't fade despite sleepless nights and indescribable danger, and the programmer downing Red Bulls to make a deadline—all have hardiness, but do they take anything away from those experiences? The one with grit, the determination to make a difference—she endures as well as the others, but then she processes that event into something that will allow her to make a bigger impact next time.

If the grind is wearing you down, then you may be viewing the grind as the enemy, something apart from the work itself. The person with grit, on the other hand, understands that the grind is part of the work, that the grind is part of what makes the work interesting, a challenge, worth doing. If there were no grind, you'd need no grit.

RESILIENCE: The dynamic process of overcoming adversity, and doing it again and again, includes both perseverance and hardiness. As the marketplace continues to create obstacles and deal setbacks, bringing grit to the problem (as a process, not as a single event) turns every obstacle into a learning process, not a momentary hassle to be dealt with.

Resilience demands flexibility—the willingness to change one thing in order to make up for something that's broken or failing.

The endless emergency of getting it over with is replaced by the daily practice of doing the work. This shift in attitude transforms the work and the worker.

AMBITION: The desire for accomplishment, power, or superiority has nothing to do with grit, except that people committed to a goal and a way of being are often given credit for having those things.

From the outside, it appears that there's causation between grit and success, but while they are correlated, they aren't necessarily connected.

Grit exists whether or not it leads to measurable external success. Grit is its own reward.

COMMITMENT: Fifty years ago, social scientist David McClelland differentiated the fairly common "need for achievement" from the attitude we describe as gritty. People with grit consciously set long-term goals that are difficult to attain and do not waver from these difficult goals, regardless of the presence of feedback.

There's more feedback in our economy and our culture today than in any other moment in human history. We don't get annual reviews any longer; our work is reviewed every time we check our e-mail, our feeds, and our dashboards. If you've sacrificed your long-term compass at the altar of instant feedback, you might enjoy some short-term achievement, but you've given up your grit.

FLOW: Something extraordinary happens when we are swallowed up by our passion, focused beyond all reason, deep into something we care about.

Best-selling author Michael Lewis found his life's work, popular writing, while a senior at Princeton, writing his thesis on a now-forgotten topic. The content didn't matter; the way he fell into it did. While he was writing, the lizard quieted, the resistance disappeared, and time slowed down. He was in it, unafraid, unimpeded, and truly alive.

What you are engrossed in isn't nearly as important as the fact of being engrossed.

True

At the bike shop, the best mechanic will spend a few extra minutes to get the wheels true.

When they're true, they don't wobble. Efficiency is increased. The wheel is round, truly round, turning without the friction and waste that come from being a little off.

The industrial economy has demanded that we be true. It pushed our parents to ensure that we would be true, and their parents before them. The economy was hungry, hungry for the compliant worker, the one who would fit his round head into the round hole, his square hands into the square holes.

And why not? To do otherwise is to mess up the machine.

We must no longer care about messing up the machine.

What's the point of connecting in a margarine-filled world without grit, without surprise, without distinction? If we smooth out the rough edges and the dark spots and there is no one different, no one who cares, no one who speaks up, we might as well go back to bed.

The connection economy demands grit; it demands that things be out of true; it demands the art of imperfection because perfect is boring, not remarkable, and because defect free often means interest free.

We don't need more stuff; we need more humanity.

The Talent Lie

It's not a lie because there's no talent out there; it's a lie because many organizations only *pretend* that they're looking for talent.

"We want talent," they say, "as long as that talent is true, productive, and predictable. We want talent if talent means more work product per dollar, more effort per day, more of what we think we're paying for. Sure, that kind of talent, send it over."

Trued talent, of course, can't change everything; it can't create a movement or break a paradigm. Trued talent isn't talent at all, because it doesn't wobble. We can't hope for a colleague or boss or employee who is one in a million and then demand that this person have no grit, do nothing to slow down the assembly line. It's one or the other: If the organization desires efficiency, it must embrace the status quo and avoid grit at all costs. On the other hand, the organization that wants growth and seeks to create value has no choice but to hire linchpins, the ones we can't live without, the ones who stand for something. People with grit.

Is It Too Late?

This might be the only question to ask right now. Is it too late to find grit, to invoke your talents (the untrued ones, the unexpected ones, the ones that scare people)?

Let's slow down for a second and ask a more difficult question first.

Who is the self in self-control?

When you are debating with yourself about a new project, a new job, or whether or not to eat that pastrami sandwich, what exactly is going on? Who, precisely, is doing the debating?

Part of you (the part that bought this book, or at least decided to read it) is painfully aware of your potential. This part of your brain seeks respect, values achievement, and knows, truly knows, that you are capable of far more than you've done so far.

The other part of your brain is afraid. The amygdala has evolved over millions of years to optimize its ability to turn you into a puddle of quivering jelly. This part of your brain has been amplified and given a free ride by the industrialists in power. We have been brainwashed by school, indoctrinated by industrial propaganda, and mesmerized by the popular media into believing that compliance is not only safe but right and necessary.

It is never too late to tip the balance between the two parts of your brain. It's never too late to redefine self-control, to change long-ingrained habits, and to do the work you're capable of.

Our culture and the connection economy have made it easier than ever (but still incredibly difficult) for you to start walking the path of the gods. It's not a cliff or a chasm; it's a stepwise path, a gradual incline, a method, bit by bit, for getting from where you are now to where you deserve to be. Dancing.

Yes, you must leap into the void. But you can always start with a little void and work your way up.

The Problem with Blaming the System

. . . is that we know the system is broken.

If you blame being late to the conference on the airline's messing up your flights, we have no sympathy because that always happens.

If you blame your poor quarterly numbers on the declining power of television advertising, we cut you no slack because we see it dying all around us.

And if you blame your lack of job prospects on the tepid demand for hardworking, competent, but replaceable workers, you haven't told us anything we didn't already know.

Blaming the system is soothing because it lets you off the hook. But when the system is broken, we wonder why you were relying on the system in the first place.

PART FOUR

Shame, Vulnerability, and Being Naked

Kryptonite Makes Superman Real

Kryptonite, of course, is to be avoided. Kryptonite, whatever your particular variety is, can kill you. It can pierce your armor and leave you helpless.

Organizational charts are filled with individual boxes connected by thin lines, each of us an interchangeable cog in a vast system of predictable behaviors. The industrialized, corporate, organized world likes it that way. Interchangeable parts, interchangeable people. Stay inside the fence!

Inside this world of boxes, the best strategy for success is to stay put, to do our best, and to wait for our box to move up the chart. Defend the box, defend the system, and mostly, make sure you keep your armor up.

This strategy feels right. Why open up to criticism, defeat, and humiliation if you can protect yourself from it?

It feels right only because we've been indoctrinated for a hundred and fifty years.

It's not right.

Without kryptonite, Superman doesn't matter, as he is without weakness, invulnerable and boring.

Avoiding Disturbing Truths

People in power and organizations that are functioning at scale rarely seek to discover truths that disturb their status quo.

The status quo is delightful. It provides a sinecure, a safe spot in which to avoid the vicissitudes of the real world. People engaged in maintaining the status quo are competent and they enjoy their competence—disturbing truths might ruin all that.

The problem for them is that it doesn't matter whether or not they *seek* these truths. The truths will find them regardless. The economy and the culture and the market will expose these truths and then work to destroy the status quo. Sooner or later, reality wins.

Artists never stop looking for the disturbing truth behind the facade. When reality arrives, they won't be surprised, because they saw it coming. Sometimes they even encouraged it to come.

If not enough people doubt you, you're not making a difference.

Art Involves Vulnerability, and the Cost of Vulnerability Might Be Shame

The industrial age brought us the safety zone of compliance, the security of doing what we were told and getting what we were promised.

It's no surprise that the combination of great pay (due to the productivity the industrial age created) and a long-evolved fear of risk (due to millions of years of surviving in the forest and the jungle) led to a magical alignment of the safety zone and the comfort zone. Hey, this new wealth-creating job—it didn't freak us out *and* we got paid.

As the industrial age fades away, though, a new safety zone, one for artists, is being created. Change is never easy, but this one is particularly difficult because it means moving away from something hardwired into each of us—the desire to fit in.

Worse, the cost of art is vulnerability. Taking responsibility and standing up and standing out make us easy targets. For many people, that vulnerability also triggers feelings of shame, which is like an exposed nerve on a wisdom tooth, something to be avoided at all costs.

The Day I Forgot My Suit

There are six hundred people downstairs, and in an hour I'll be onstage, their invited speaker. Getting dressed this morning, I realize that I've forgotten to bring my suit jacket.

I have a good excuse—it was a hundred degrees when I left the house; who wears a suit in weather like this? But still . . .

I'm not normally anxious before I give a talk. I've given more than a thousand of them, and after a while the fear wears off. But today I'm feeling out of sorts.

The suit is a form of armor for me, like the slides, the clicker, and the edge of the stage. It protects me from intimacy. The suit labels me as the speaker, the other, the guy who is insulated from you, even if only by an eighth of an inch of fabric.

Have I disrespected the audience by not dressing better than they did? Am I ashamed to go stand up and share my vision for what they might do next? What right do I have to say anything at all to these talented practitioners of their craft?

My work is always about connecting with the audience, and that connection brings vulnerability with it. *Here I am*, I have to say. Here is what *I* think, not what someone else said, not what some study said.

And to do it half naked like this, on the edge of shame, makes that vulnerability even more pronounced for me. Not because I need to stand up and say, "Hey, everyone, I feel stupid; I'm not wearing my jacket." No, that's not what vulnerability is. It's about the story in my head, not the one I tell to the audience. It's about being willing to stand up in front of people and own what I have to say.

That's part of why it's worth doing. To do it as an invulnerable superhero would mean nothing to me and less to the audience.

"Don't Fix Me; Love Me for What's Broken"

The prospect of shame can easily paralyze us. When our friend shares a litany of problems and explains why he's stuck (the lawsuit, the difficulty raising money, the yoga injury, the problem relationship with Dad), it's entirely likely that he's not asking for a solution; he's asking for empathy and understanding.

But why won't he try to fix his problems? Perhaps they have become a crutch, a companion, perhaps a best friend for him now.

Why not lean forward and use every tool available to take the huge steps to actually go forward?

Because forward is risky, and forward might not work, and forward might not be better than this. Sure, all of that is true, but most of all: Going forward might open the door to being thought a fool, to being guilty of hubris, and most of all, to exposing himself to the shame of trying and failing.

Again and again we've been deceived, brainwashed into believing that perfection is more important than effort, and sold on the idea that we have to settle for what's been offered.

Art Is Vulnerability Without the Prospect of Shame

Kamiwaza involves removing artifice and defense and poses from our work and boiling it down to the true essence, performing it in a way that eliminates hiding places and excuses.

Which makes us extraordinarily vulnerable.

After we've not only given our all but done it in a way that leaves us nowhere to point the finger, then of course the results belong to us.

No cog in the industrial system chooses to do this. The system offers us protection, a policy, an excuse. To own the idea, to be responsible for the project . . . we risk being shamed for our arrogance.

The industrialists amplified the shame of hubris to keep us in line.

The easiest way to ensure that kids do their homework is to publicly shame the student who doesn't do his. When those in power want to ensure that the masses buy what they sell, they shame those who apparently can't afford to buy what they need to fit in. The easiest way to ensure conformity among employees is to single out the outliers and shame them for their temerity, for their disobedience, or for being uppity.

The cycle of shame starts early and it never lets up. They use shame to keep conversations and behaviors in the closet and to ensure that those without anointed and clear power keep quiet. Accusations like "How dare you?" and "Who do you think you are?" and "How presumptuous!" cut right to the core.

When someone in power says, "Why did you do this?" we've been trained to respond, "Because I was told to." This is apparently a safe answer, a defense against responsibility. "I was doing my job" is supposed to insulate us from shame.

Fear of shame is a powerful tool to modify behavior, and those in power have been using it for years. They want to be able to change us by delivering shame, and we've been taught to listen to it, believe it, and swallow it.

It's not easy to expose ourselves to that much potential shame, so the only alternative is to refuse to accept the shame and merely honor the connections made instead. It's fine to acknowledge that there are those who will seek to shame you, but that doesn't mean you have to accept what's given. We don't work for the applause, and we'd be foolish to read the anonymous comments on Amazon or the tweets coming from the back of the room. When your restaurant gets a lousy review on Yelp or a stranger yells something out the window, that attempt to get you to quiet down and conform doesn't belong to you unless you want it to.

No, the person with *kamiwaza* says to the person on the other end, "This is me." And in response, we open the door to a valid human connection with the person who is generous enough to receive our work the way that we meant to deliver it.

But if we allow shame to be part of our vulnerability, we allow it to destroy our work. Shame is the fatal black hole, the third rail, the wire that none of us wants to touch. If your vulnerability feels like it is getting you close to that dark place, you'll back off and put up your armor.

It's impossible to do art with stakes that high. You can't say, "If it works, fine, but if it fails, I'm shamed."

No, the only way to be successfully vulnerable is to separate the results of your art from your instinct to feel shamed. And that's possible, because while someone can attempt to shame you, shame must also be accepted to be effective. We can't make you feel shame without your participation.

Shameless?

What a crushing indictment. To call someone shameless is to cast them in the role of a pariah, the one who refuses to play by our culture's rules. The shameless self-promoter, the shameless hussy, the shameless and craven rip-off artist . . .

And yet there's a different way to be shameless.

This is the person with so much to give that she's both willing to be vulnerable to the audience and sidestepping the dark feelings of shame at the same time.

To stand onstage or at the meeting or behind the keyboard and to do your work shamelessly is to do it with godlike confidence. Not because people won't offer you shame but because you will refuse to accept it.

In the words of Edmund Bergler, "the megalomaniac pleasure of creation . . . produces a type of elation which cannot be compared with that experienced by other mortals." Elation because we combine the risk of vulnerability with the immortal ability to be shameless.

Shame Has Long Been a Tool of Those in Power

Tribes seek to shame those who act or look different.

Schools use shame to force compliance on those who might speak up.

Shame is easily amplified, as it's hardwired into us. Even a puppy knows how to put a look of shame on his face.

When those in power use shame to bully the weak into compliance, they are stealing from us. They tell us that they will expose our secrets (not good enough, not hardworking enough, not from the right family, made a huge mistake once) and will use the truth to exile us from our tribe.

This shame, the shame that lives deep within each of us, is used as a threat. And when those in power use it, they take away part of our humanity.

Accepting Shame (or Not)

The downside of seeing and making and communicating is the shame that's sometimes offered back to you.

One way the community responds to a courageous act is by

seeking to shame the courageous one. Instead of rewarding you for caring enough to try, they work to silence you by creating shame.

Shame is the soul killer, the enemy of those who would have courage. Shame is the emotion that is handed to you when you are called out for what you've done or what you've said.

The easiest way to avoid shame (which is something that every single breathing human wants to do) is to lie low. If you don't speak up and don't act out, it's unlikely that you'll be singled out to be shamed. *But lying low is now a recipe for ending up far outside your safety zone.* The industrial economy sold you on the bargain that avoiding attention meant avoiding shame and that obedience led to stability. While you can still avoid shame by hiding, you won't find happiness or even stability that way.

The thing is, shame is a choice. It's worth repeating: Shame can't be forced on you; it must be accepted.

The artist, then, combines courage with a fierce willingness to refuse to accept shame. Blame, sure. Shame, never.

Where is the shame in using our best intent to make art for those we care about?

Did It Work?

I almost let reviews and comments destroy my work.

I was so worried about unanimous feedback, about reaching everyone, that it paralyzed me.

A few years ago, I gave a speech to twelve thousand people. I had prepared for almost a year and presented a talk with entirely new material, a talk that was heartfelt and important to me. It ended with a huge standing ovation and great feedback from people I cared about.

On the way to the airport, I checked Twitter to see what people thought. With twelve thousand people in the room, there were, no surprise, a bunch of tweets. More than a hundred had been posted in the few minutes since I had gotten off the stage. And one, just one, was negative.

Guess what I spent the whole time thinking about on the way home?

Writing is a lonely business, and after a book is published, many authors look for validation. We check the Amazon best-seller ranks, the reviews in *Publishers Weekly*, and our Amazon reviews as they appear. We read the comments on our blog posts and see if anyone has said something about our work on Twitter.

There's no economic rationale here, because there's no economic connection at all between these bits of feedback and the check that might or might not show up in a year's time. No, this is about ego, about the lizard brain, and about fortifying ourselves to do it again.

The first thing I noted about the reviews in *Publishers Weekly* (which are syndicated, quite prominently, on every Amazon page and are ostensibly read by booksellers deciding what to carry in their stores) was that they were anonymous. The second was that they generally disliked my best work and weren't shy about questioning its worth. Then I noticed that they were wrong—if the goal was to tell booksellers what was going to actually sell, they weren't doing a very good job with my books or with the works of a bunch of other popular authors.

Then I realized what I was doing with the comments and reviews I was reading. I would read thirty of them, and twenty-nine would be positive (sometimes extraordinarily so) and one would be a direct hit job, a brutal takedown of who I was and what I was trying to do. And for the next few days, all that my lizard brain would let me think about was the bad one. No writing got done at that point, just more search for validation. A terrible cycle, of course, because looking for more validation brought me face to face with more dismissal, too.

I was amplifying the negative at the expense of the positive, not to serve any useful function, not to make my writing better, but to destroy it. The lizard brain, so attuned to people laughing behind our backs, was on high alert for this sort of criticism and would do anything it could to stop me from writing again.

I haven't sought out and read a review or a tweet since. This is not cowardice; it's the act of someone who wants to keep writing and is determined to do it for an audience of his choosing.

Shun the nonbelievers.

Whom Should the Artist Care About?

The watchword of the sane artist: *Shun the nonbelievers*.

First you must pick yourself, and then you choose your audience.

After you've created your art, whatever it is—a service, an idea, an interaction, a performance, a meeting—it's done. What the audience does with it is out of your control.

If you focus your angst and emotion on the people who don't get it, you've destroyed part of your soul and haven't done a thing to improve your art. Your art, if you made it properly, wasn't for them in the first place. Worse, the next time you make art, those nonbelievers will be the ones at the front of your mind.

When Patrick McGoohan traded in his reputation as a James Bond–type actor to produce and star in *The Prisoner*, he was taking a huge leap. He traded in his reputation to get creative control over a new series. He then went ahead and invented a TV show that almost no one "got."

Which was fine with him, because it wasn't *for* everyone. It was for a few. Forty years later, his show, unlike all of its competition, is still discussed, still watched, still connects.

The kind of art I'm describing doesn't seek to please the masses. The masses (by definition) aren't pleased by the new; they are pleased by what others think. *Harry Potter*'s first fans were enthralled by the art that J. K. Rowling challenged them with. The next hundred million readers embraced a mass cultural phenomenon, not an unproven book from an unknown author. The book didn't change, but its role as a risky piece of art did.

That doesn't mean you have no one who decides to judge you. An unheard symphony isn't a symphony; it is notes on paper. Art doesn't become art until it meets an audience. *Your goal as an artist is to make art that moves the audience of your choice.*

If your efforts fail to move the audience you've chosen, then you should learn what worked and what didn't and incorporate that knowledge into your next effort. Interact with the audience if it helps you learn to do better next time, but not if it gives the resistance an excuse to destroy your future art.

Only a self-negating artist reads his Amazon reviews and the Twitter feedback on his work. He will learn nothing and will amplify his lizard brain's certainty of his worthlessness.

Figure out who your art is for, get better at connecting with that audience, and ignore the rest.

Artists lead, they don't chase.

All the Things You Can't Talk About

Make a list. Make a list of the things you can't talk about at work or with your spouse or with others you care about.

The things on this list (and those that you were hesitant to even write down) point to places where you or the organization feel shame. These hot buttons are places where you'd prefer to be invulnerable. These are areas where you build armor, where you don't want anyone to go.

Armor prevents connection, and shame festers. The shadow of shame kills art.

When you talk about these things, when you own them, shame starts to lose its power, and vulnerability becomes available to you again.

True Connection

With our true friends we don't talk over dinner about which place did a good job detailing the SUV or even how we're going to get ahead at work. We talk about our hopes and our dreams and our fears. We let down our guard, set aside our armor, and open ourselves up. We're vulnerable and trusting and willing to speak (and to hear) the truth.

When those who love you speak of a life well lived, we'll talk about the lines you managed to color outside of, the people you touched, and the ruckus you made. Most of all, we'll remember how you took a chance and connected with us.

If Your Audience Seeks to Shame You for the Art You Make

Then they are no longer your audience, and they don't deserve your vulnerability. The life of an artist requires interaction with the audience, and so we have to choose an audience that respects our work. Not because it's easier that way but because only by exchanging gifts and dignity can we do our best work.

It's not good enough.

I'm not good enough.

It's the best I can do.

It's real and it's generous.

Let's try.

This might work.

Rowing Someone Else's Boat

There is nothing wrong with a boss, with organizations, with aligning with those who share your goals and working together to reach them.

But one of the remnants of the industrial age is the cultural imperative to take on what was important to our overseers. If others are busy deciding which metrics ought to matter to you, you have given up something precious indeed.

And we all have overseers. We have banks or managers or bosses. We have audiences or critics or mothers-in-law. The moment we give up our internal compass in exchange for satisfying the cultural need to follow the leader, we've made someone else the boss.

Money or status or the power to boss others around—are these the things you truly want, or are they stand-ins for something else? In school we teach kids to earn high scores and to comply and to meet the standards of their teachers and parents. But what if those things aren't part of *your* agenda?

At the very same time that the economy is shifting and the fence is coming down and the rules are changing, people are starting to wake up and realize that they don't have to want what the system wants them to want.

Musicians and the Boat

David Byrne stopped being part of Talking Heads. He walked away from rock-star status, from sold-out arenas, from the ability to put a hit on the pop charts. Those were someone else's dreams, and he chose not to live someone else's life any longer.

Byrne didn't stop making art. Far from it. He went back to making *his* art, the art he chose to make, not the show the market was insisting he make. He has written books on traveling by bicycle, written essays about the architecture of Atlanta, and produced a successful series of records featuring Brazilian music. Not famous art but important art.

Peter Gabriel was also riding as high as a rock star could, issuing one gold record after another. But for him, churning out another pop anthem was no longer a risk, no longer a human place. So he stopped. He began working with Amnesty International and then started a groundbreaking human-rights organization called WIT-NESS.

The goal for these men wasn't to enrich their record labels or to please the fans who hardly knew them. It was to continue to explore the edges of their passions and to do work they had never done before.

The permeability of the postindustrial society, the leverage we have to reach out to those with similar goals, and most of all, the value that real art creates—all of these things work together to hand us the freedom to decide our own course and to maximize our own value, in whatever direction we choose.

If you're in the business of making and strengthening connections, there isn't just one way to do your work.

Starting now, is your goal the same as that of the stock-market pickers and profit maximizers? Do you define your work by how much money you've earned or how much stuff you've purchased? Reality TV offers us the dream of fame at the expense of our dignity. The fashionistas in high school want to judge you by your outfit, and the skeptic cares how famous your college was.

Stop.

It's not for them to decide what your art is.

Four Common Mistakes That Help You Hide

Busy is the same as brave.

A mentor is going to change your life.

Waiting to get picked is the next step.

There is a secret, and you will soon learn it.

Stop Pretending You're Not Special

Where did the special demarcation come from, and why did you end up on the wrong side of it?

Of course you're special. You're capable of doing something no one has ever done before, able to see something no one has ever seen before. How could you not be?

But can we all be special? The cynic says that if everyone is special, no one is.

No, the label isn't an accurate description of who you are (or aren't). The label of "special" describes what you do, not who you are. We're all special in our own way the moment we choose to be.

And Now the Resistance Arrives

The lizard brain, the hot-wired, fire-breathing voice that's fast but stupid, is responsible for fear, quick action, anger, and part of our sex drive. All the things you'd want to have working well if you were hoping for individual and species survival in a dangerous place.

Over time, we've advanced our situation so much that most of us don't actually live in dangerous places any longer. But the amygdala is still there, activated in the rare moments when we need it, as when we're getting mugged in an alley or we're on the prowl in a singles bar. Unfortunately, it's also activated whenever we're about to create worthwhile art.

Brilliant author Steve Pressfield has given this activation a name. He calls it the resistance.

The resistance is the confused and angry noise in our heads that shows up whenever we put our creativity on the line. It is writer's block and procrastination and, most insidious of all, the subtle instinct to do a little less, to polish along the edges, to fit in, to get along, to become mediocre.

The voice of the resistance is a million years old. It understands that art is dangerous, because art makes you vulnerable, because art generates criticism, because your art is not for everyone.

Back in the distant antediluvian past, criticism was dangerous indeed. The outlier got noticed . . . and not often in a good way.

Today, though, as we've seen, art is our best (and sometimes only) option for success. And art comes with a naturally limiting emotion—the resistance wants to stop it.

When you complain to me that you're feeling the resistance, I don't feel bad for you. I'm thrilled. I'm thrilled because the resistance isn't like a sprained ankle or some other malady we seek to avoid when working out. The resistance is the shadow of art. No art, no resistance.

Yves Klein surprised the avant-garde art world with the doctored photo of him (on the next page) on a side street in Paris.

I've looked at this photo a thousand times and actually tried to get the rights to put it on the cover of this book. Notice where Klein is facing. This is not a man intent on self-harm. It is someone comfortable with the void, eager to see what he will discover. He has not been deceived by some propaganda about Icarus. There is somewhere he wants to go, and if it means facing down the void to get there, he's in.

Of course you're feeling the resistance. That's a good thing, a symptom that you're close to doing something that matters. There's no doubt that you're feeling it.

The real question is: What are you going to do about the resistance?

There's No War of Art

Pressfield's essential book about the resistance is called *The War of Art*. And the title is something that he and I disagree about.

The resistance cannot be productively fought to the death.

135

There can be no war on the resistance because you cannot win it, and starting a war you can't win is foolish.

Once I realized that the cold sweat, the palpitations, the wily stalling, the insecurity, and the fear were part of making art, I was able to relax into my work. It's not even a cease-fire any longer. It's a partnership, not a war.

When the resistance shows up, I know that I'm winning. Not my fight against it, but my fight to make art.

Terrific, It's Here

The resistance is a symptom that you're on the right track. *The resistance is not something to be avoided; it's something to seek out.*

That's the single most important sentence in this book.

The artist seeks out the feeling of the resistance and then tries to maximize it.

The cog, the day laborer, the compliant student—they seek to eliminate the feeling instead.

That's the choice.

Change your mind, right now, not later. If you determine that you will see better, make better, and most of all, dare to turn your tabula rasa into something frightening, that's when you will begin to live the life of the artist. And the artist's constant companion is the screaming lizard brain.

If it goes away, you have to change your work until it returns.

The resistance pushes you to refuse to believe in its existence.

The skepticism you're feeling about the impact of the lizard brain on your art is a natural side effect of the amygdala's ability to protect itself. If your frontal lobe is unaware that you're being sabotaged, it's less likely to do the hard work of putting yourself at risk.

Change Your Mind

Artists fail, and failing means that sometimes you need to change your mind about what you thought the best path might be. That's one reason that failure is anathema—it means we have to change our minds.

The real problem when working with a consultant, a therapist, or a coach isn't that we don't know what to do. The real problem is that we don't want to change our mind.

It's a skill, an attribute of those who are successful and happy. If you need a pro to help you, that's great, but be clear with yourself that the goal isn't to find a better path; it's to find the bravery to change your mind.

Fun, Easy, and Reliable

Those seem like good attributes of a career path. The industrialists who sold you propaganda about Icarus, and about fitting in and getting a "good" job, pitch all three attributes.

Art offers none of them.

While there are moments of fun, the most important part of the artist's day is when she comes face to face with the resistance. Real art isn't easy to create; it's the hardest thing in the world, which is why it's so scarce. When we get to the difficult part, the part that matters, it's so much more fun and so much less effort to back off and call it a day.

And reliable? Flying too close to the sun has significant risks, and they show up all the time.

What Does "Yes" Look Like?

My colleague Steve Dennis has been in charge of innovation and strategy at two different *Fortune* 500 companies. He writes,

> More often than not, when our team has gone to the CEO or the Board asking for support to move ahead, we were told "no." Sometimes we understood why we were declined and walked away with clear feedback and a road-map to move forward. Other times the feedback could be summed up by either "this is not the right time" or "we'll know a great idea when we see it."
>
> Just because you have risen to a senior leadership position doesn't necessarily mean it's any easier to walk through your fear. Frankly it's a hell of a lot easier to say "no" to a new venture than to risk being wrong or looking foolish.
>
> As leaders we can do better than defaulting to the least risky position, to letting our lizard brain win. If we are going to say "no" we need to know what a "yes" looks like. And we need to be able to communicate that to those we lead.
>
> And when they come back having addressed our concerns and resolved our doubts, then we owe them that "yes."

It takes guts to say yes, and you owe it to your team to be clear and consistent about what earns a "yes." Your job is to use your guts, not to hide them.

No One Knows Anything

William Goldman said that about the film business, but it's true about your business as well.

Kids' books are a great example. Every parent figures he has at least one book for toddlers in him—how hard could it be? All you have to do is follow the template and get picked by a book editor.

But it *is* hard. It's hard because every successful kids' book is a breakthrough. Every book that works breaks the rules that came before it; every one is a surprise to someone who encounters it for the first time.

You need to know the conventional wisdom inside and out. Not to obey the rules, but to break them.

Defining Your Audience

"Just because you made some art doesn't mean we care."

This is one of the many heartbreaks of art. You toil and sacrifice and expose yourself, and yet you hear, "Someone cares, perhaps, but not us."

Rejection says something about the critic, but not about you. Perhaps it means you chose the wrong audience. And yes, perhaps, if you've exhausted all possible audiences, it means that you need to make better art.

I'm walking a fine line here, and I know it. I'm suggesting that the masses are not your audience; a weird segment of the population is. But at the same time, just because you think you're brilliant, or you've sacrificed, or you've faced down the lizard brain, this doesn't guarantee that you've made anything good. Your effort is rarely correlated with how much the audience cares.

The eye of the needle here is small indeed. Your puzzle is to find an idea or a product or an interaction that touches the right person, in the right way, at precisely the right moment.

The connection economy delivers access to more people, in new ways, than have ever been available to you before. You get to set the stage, you get to decide whom the interaction is for (to a point), and you get to choose the outcome you seek.

All that choice gives you leverage, but it also raises the bar. "Is this the best you can do?"

That's a daunting question, but with the tools you've been given, it's a fair one.

The Deception Sells You on Mass

Of course, you've been taught that the masses are all that matter, that critics are smart, that you have no right (none) to do something outside the mainstream. The very nature of that phrase, "outside the mainstream," brings so much value judgment with it.

More applause is always better. It's better to be on TV, better to be on national TV, better to be famous. If you insist on starting something, better to have it well funded, and better still to have it well funded by someone we've heard of. Better to have an approved job, a stellar résumé, and the approval of all the people who matter. And they matter because the masses revere their power and wealth and authority.

This system, of course, was invented by those in power. It exists to maintain their power, not to encourage you to do the art you're capable of.

Gambling with People

I had a gambling addiction with people's opinions of me. When someone says, "I don't like that guy," I like to sit down and talk to him, and make sure he's not misunderstanding me, and sometimes you can save it. So it only makes sense that I would scale that up to a million. And as soon as I'd get it back to even, I started making big bets again. What I didn't realize was that one of the best things you can do is walk away. I've arrived at something that I wish I'd known a long time ago, which is that *I have to let people not respect me.*

—John Mayer, *Rolling Stone*, 2012

The audience you choose might be everyone, infinity, the mass of humanity. And you can't please everyone. You can decide to please the readers of *Us*, *Rolling Stone*, *Time*, the *National Enquirer*, and *Playboy*. You can put on your show for the entire Internet if you want.

And a big enough audience will destroy you. Some people in that large audience want it taller, shorter, wider, thinner, cheaper, more expensive, faster, or slower. The only choice you have if you want to continue is to ignore those who don't get the joke. Part of your hard work is to shun the nonbelievers and to focus on the audience of your choice. The mass marketers and the industrialists need everyone. You don't. You merely need to matter to a few.

The dangerous addiction is to keep expanding the audience until we find people who hate our work.

And then our reflex is to listen to those people, to the haters, to the exclusion of those we sought to serve in the first place.

Performance Anxiety

It's silly and counterproductive to worry as your boss reads your report, or as the audience files in to hear your concerto. The work is already done.

Take what you need and leave the rest. Just be careful in understanding exactly what it is you need.

Their reaction isn't yours; it belongs to them. The art is yours.

PART FIVE

To Make Art, Think Like an Artist. To Connect, Be Human.

"Make Good Art"

"Make good art" is Neil Gaiman's prescription for whatever ails you. If the job market isn't there, if your boss doesn't respect you, if the world doesn't get you—make good art.

If it's not working, then make better art.

If you don't know how to make better art, learn.

If the people around you are sabotaging your art, ignore them.

If your boss stops your art, make different art. If he stops it again, take responsibility and make different art. Keep doing it until your art gets better or you get fired, whichever happens first.

And then make more art.

Your art at first will be timid. It might not be based on a truly clear awareness of the world, because the lizard brain will cloud your sight in order to protect itself.

But day by day, project by project, you can train yourself to ship.

Ship small art. Then ship medium art. Then ship world-changing, scary, change-your-underwear art.

The Three Foundations of Art

Author James Elkins writes of the three components necessary for someone to become an artist: seeing, making, and the tabula rasa.

First, students need to learn to see. They have to see the world as it is, without labels, without knowing the name of what is seen.

Second, they are taught how to make. How to use hands or voice or body to take what they see and reflect it back to the world.

And third, and most difficult, the artist starts with a blank slate. Art must be done for the first time, not repeated, and that first stroke, those first words—this is the source of our fear. How can we not be vulnerable when the work is ours, not that of another?

Steve Martin embraced the three steps. He *saw*, over decades behind the magic counter at Disneyland, on the stage at Knott's Berry Farm, and traveling from club to club, how audience members interacted with one another, with the venue, and with him.

He *made*. He kept obsessive journals. He tested and measured and repeated. Three shows a night was normal, hundreds of shows a year, year after year.

Most of all, he relentlessly stuck to his blank slate. Theft was so rare for him that in his autobiography he singles out each and every time he borrowed a line from a mentor—always with their permission first. The rest of his act, the rest of his work, was determinedly original. Martin's routine seems obvious now, trivial even, but when he created it, it was brave and new.

Don't think! Thinking is the enemy of creativity. It's self-conscious, and anything self-conscious is lousy. You can't try to do things. You simply must do things.

—Ray Bradbury

First, Learn to See

Our preconceptions and our fear conspire to make it difficult to see the world as it is.

Buddhists call it *prajna*—accepting reality as it occurs instead of interpreting it as part of our ongoing narrative. Duke Stump insists that you "quiet your cleverness." The trick isn't coming up with an interpretation of events that allows you to maintain your worldview; it is to accept what happens without stopping to interpret it according to your biases.

Fred Wilson is one of our most successful venture capitalists precisely because of his ability to see. He saw that Delicious and Twitter and dozens of other companies had commercial potential. Clive Davis was the genius who discovered or promoted Whitney Houston, Patti Smith, the Outlaws, Dionne Warwick, Aretha Franklin, Carly Simon, the Grateful Dead, the Kinks, and Lou Reed. He didn't always make the records or sell the records. He saw (and heard) the potential in the musicians around him.

The ability to see the market and the technology and the talent as it is, instead of how you want it to be (or fear it to be), is one of the secret skills of the successful creator.

Alan Webber and Bill Taylor were among the dozens of talented editors who had worked at the *Harvard Business Review*, but they were the only two editors focused enough to see the business revolution that they chronicled in *Fast Company*, one of the most important (and profitable) magazines ever published.

It comes with practice. The right kind of practice, though. Make predictions based on what you see. Write them down. "Someone is going to make an app that lets people share pictures." "The Yelp IPO is going to be very successful." "This new employee is going to break all her sales targets within two months."

After we read just two issues of *Fast Company*, suddenly the economy and the future came into focus for some of us. And Alan and Bill saw it first and explained it to us.

When you're wrong, the instinct is to blame the universe, not your worldview. We rarely want to surrender our framework for how things work or question our assumptions. Instead, we rail against fate or chalk it up to random noise. Instead, every misjudgment is a chance to revisit and hone our ability to notice the underlying needs in the market, the forces at work in success and failure.

Notice

Every time I walk into a bookstore, I notice things. I notice typography. Pricing. The thickness of books and the type of cover stock being used. I notice where the salespeople are standing and how smart they are. I notice the guy on the couch, buying nothing but reading a lot. What's he reading? I eavesdrop on conversations, listen in on what's being hand sold.

Paco Underhill has turned noticing into an art. His company, Envirosell, monitors tens of thousands of hours of silent retail-store security-camera footage, noticing how people shop. Women, for example, don't like it if another shopper brushes against them while they're browsing. So Paco persuaded a client to widen the aisles (oh no, less inventory!) to eliminate the butt brush. The result? Increased revenue even though there were fewer items for sale.

Woody Guthrie was the most important folk singer of the twentieth century. But before he accomplished that, he visited forty-five states, learned tens of thousands of songs, and immersed himself in native and immigrant cultures. Without that foundation, he would never have had the tools to create his art.

The difficult part of seeing is setting aside what you're sure you already know. When the Web was young, I was already an "expert." I had built successful online promotions and run them on Prodigy, AOL, and CompuServe. So I knew what I was talking about. Or at least I thought I did.

Browsing around online in 1993, I didn't see. All I could understand about the Web was that it was free, slow, clunky, and without a center. Of course it wasn't going to work. Every dumb stunt I saw online reinforced my skepticism, and of course I ignored the successes that contradicted my worldview.

That year, instead of starting a search engine, a chat site, or an online auction site, I wrote a book about clever stuff you could find online. I made eighty thousand dollars. The guys who started Yahoo!, on the other hand, with the same investment I made, ended up creating about eighty billion dollars in value (a million times more than I did) with the same information.

We both had access to the same resources and to the same technology. The difference is that David and Jerry saw something that I refused to see, because I was too clever to see it.

You can't accurately see until you abandon your worldview. Your worldview is incredibly useful in everyday life—it's the set of assumptions, biases, and beliefs you bring to the interactions you have with the world, and it saves a lot of time. Because you don't have to come to new conclusions after each interaction, it's easier to process familiar inputs and easier to be consistent.

But your worldview, by its nature, keeps you from seeing the world as it is.

A lifetime spent noticing begins to turn into the ability to see what others can't.

What You Choose to See

On my phone is a game called Shanghai. It uses little domino-like tiles, each with a symbol, and the object is to find matches and clear the board. When I started playing this game, it took me about sixteen minutes to clear the entire thing at the standard level.

As I practiced (okay, as I wasted time on long flights), my times got better. I started recognizing the symbols without naming them. I stopped saying, "Uh, okay, there's the thing with two *M*'s on it. . . . Is there another one? Wait, there's the red sword. . . ." I got better at seeing deeply into the game board and noticing the patterns. It didn't take long for me to get my time to less than eight minutes on a regular basis.

While this is nothing to be particularly proud of, what it demonstrates to me is how we're able to learn to recognize patterns. It's not something you need to be born with; it's something you can learn.

And so a car guy learns to tell the difference between a car design that's going to sell and one that's not. And a cop learns to recognize the symptoms of behavior that might lead to trouble.

Until they don't. At some point, we stop seeing patterns and start looking for shortcuts. We profile, believing our own shortcuts to be correct, and so everything gets a name.

We profile because it speeds things up, but mostly we profile because it's safer. We don't have to risk experiencing things if we can merely remind ourselves of previous experiences. Not only that, but if we preprocess our reactions to things already labeled, we don't have to reconsider our plans. "I know how to hit this kind of pitch" is very similar to "I don't like those kinds of people." The former helps us improve our batting average, while the latter destroys any chance we have of making a useful connection.

Seeing Is Forgetting the Name of the Thing One Sees

Successful people are good at assigning labels. Accurately labeling people and situations and ideas makes it easier to process them faster and with leverage. If you know the difference between a snake and a stick, you're a lot less likely to get bitten.

The problem with labels is that once they're applied, it's impossible to see what lies beneath. When the world changes, then, our labels cease to function and we're blind to the opportunities that are presenting themselves.

Artists learn to see all over again. They learn to forgo labels and bring the fresh instead.

Art is the act of pointing a light at the darkness. Before you turn on the light, you have no idea what you're about to see, and once you know what you're going to see, it's no longer dark.

Many Shades of White

Here's what happens when domain knowledge is used to enhance our ability to see:

> Look at that wall carefully and you'll of course see that its whiteness is not of just one tone. The light is streaming in from the window, so that it's a brighter white to that side, fading into grays over to this side. There are blues and greens and even purples. It's a little bit more difficult to see the incidental transitions, the low-grade shadows caused by the varying textures, because of the starkness of the contrast between the white wall and the black plank.
>
> —Robert Irwin, conceptual artist

Most of us see a white wall, if we see anything at all. A gifted painter sees a rainbow. And the talented author finds the words, paradoxically, to label the rainbow.

Our Eyes Don't Lie . . .

But our brain does. All the time. Our worldview changes what we see and how we interpret what we learn, making us blind. And we are blind to our blindness.

People change their opinions about fashion or politics or food depending on whom they are listening to or what party they think originated an idea. The price of a bottle of wine has a direct impact on how good even the most discerning wine experts say it tastes.

The placebo effect has an impact on more than medicine—*we see what we believe, not the other way around.*

Rarely do we see the world as it is. Most of the time we are so busy compartmentalizing, judging, and ignoring what we can't abide that we see almost nothing. We don't see opportunities. We fail to see pain. And most of all, we refuse to see the danger in doing nothing.

If you can't see, you will never make art successfully.

Ask a Colleague

If a piece of art in the marketplace is working to change things and you don't know why, ask a colleague to explain it to you. If people are listening to or watching or buying something and you don't get it, inquire as to why. If a blog post or a novel or a strategy makes no sense to you, ask someone who knows.

Learn to see through their eyes.

Why does this brand outsell that one? How come we have this policy? What's broken about this interface? Shouldn't this cost less than that?

If you don't have a colleague to ask, get one. If your colleague isn't as smart as you, teach him until he is.

The goal isn't to adopt a few new pattern rules or to memorize some new labels. The goal is to have so many pattern rules and so many labels and be aware of so many worldviews that they swirl together and allow you to become naive all over again.

To be naive is to abandon your hard-earned worldview. It means seeing the world without prejudice and accepting it as it is, as opposed to the way you're expecting it to be.

Second, Learn to Make

Everyone should learn to code.

Not because we have a tremendous shortage of people who can produce things in [insert the name of your favorite hot programming language here] but because once you know how to make something, it changes how you see things. Once you know how to set lead type, typography looks different. Once you know how to assemble an electronic device, every computer seems a bit less mysterious. Once you know how to give a speech, you see things in the speeches others give.

Learning how to make things turns you from a spectator into a participant, from someone at the mercy of the system to someone who is helping to run the system.

Learning how to make gives you the guts to make more, to fail more often, to get better at making.

We Have Insulated Our Kids from Making

There are no user-serviceable parts inside.

Don't color outside the lines.

Play with your video game; it's too hot to play outside.

It's cheaper to buy a new one than it is to fix this one, and anyway, we don't have a soldering iron.

What's a soldering iron?

In the spectator-fueled industrial economy, there were a few who made and the rest of us watched. In the connection economy, on the other hand, we're spending more and more time consuming what our peers make and then turning right around and making things for our friends to consume.

If you are afraid to write or edit or assemble or disassemble, you are merely a spectator. And you are trapped, trapped by the instructions of those you've chosen to follow. Twenty people in the field and eighty thousand in the stands. The spectators are the ones who paid to watch, but it's the players on the field who are truly alive.

Three Useless Questions

Where do you get your ideas?
What sort of software do you use to do your writing?
What should I do next?

The answers don't matter. At all. The choice of tools doesn't matter; the method doesn't matter. You don't need a guru; you need experience, the best kind of experience, the experience of repeated failure.

You need the good taste to see your own work for what it is, and you earn that taste not only not by emulating those who made art before you but by failing, by repeatedly discovering what works and what doesn't.

And Then You Bomb

John Carter is a terrible movie, a movie most American filmgoers can tell is terrible after watching any twelve seconds of it. It's so terrible it caused the Walt Disney Company film division to lose money.

On the other hand, it set box-office records in Russia. If Russia had been the desired audience, it wouldn't have been terrible at all.

How did Andrew Stanton, who did such a magnificent job of making films like *Finding Nemo*, get this one so totally wrong?

It's not that he doesn't know how to make a movie. It's not that he didn't have support. The problem is that he didn't see the film the way most American filmgoers saw it. It turns out that for a live-action film, Andrew Stanton sees like a Russian, and it turns out that in his artistic frenzy and dedication, he refused to listen to Disney colleagues who saw what he refused to see.

This is an expensive lesson to learn on a movie that cost about a quarter of a billion dollars to make, but it's a lesson all makers have to learn. We see, we make, and then we repeat.

Domain Knowledge

Is this joke funny?

> Heisenberg looks around the bar and says, "Because there are three of us and because this is a bar, it must be a joke. But the question remains, is it funny or not?"
>
> And Gödel thinks for a moment and says, "Well, because we're inside the joke, we can't tell whether it's funny. We'd have to be outside looking at it."
>
> And Chomsky looks at both of them and says, "Of course it's funny. You're just telling it wrong."

The only way to know whether the joke is funny is to have at least a passing acquaintance with the reputations of the three men sitting in the bar. Domain knowledge can fill us with expectation, calcify our worldview, and make it difficult to see the world as it is. But it can also fill in the blanks and enable us to understand how something works and to know enough about how to make it better.

Bob Dylan knows more about the history of American music

than anyone you have ever met. Fred Wilson can describe the details of a thousand successful venture investments. Eileen Fisher can look at a garment and instantly tell you who inspired it. This knowledge isn't the side effect of doing important work for a generation. This is an important foundation that makes it possible to do important work. Andrew Stanton has world-class domain knowledge when it comes to animated film. His expensive error was being sure that his taste was as correct when it came to live-action films.

Please understand this about my example: Many academics know plenty about Chomsky or Gödel, but they've relentlessly avoided doing the hard work of making art. Knowledge is not sufficient. It's necessary but not enough.

Finally, Learn to Embrace the Blank Slate

The first thing the consultant wants to know is, "What's your budget?"

The second thing she asks is, "What do you think you should do?"

This might be a good way to make the sale to an organization that already knows what it wants. It's not clear that this is a good way to start a discussion that leads to real and significant growth.

The blank slate is a requirement for original art. If you merely rehash what came before, if you offer me the same hot dog you served me yesterday, the same direct-mail letter you sold me last week, the same search engine I used last month, then nothing remarkable has happened; no connection has been made.

Of course the form and the boundaries don't change each time. No one wants the local bar to become a bowling alley tomorrow

155

and a strip club the next day. Art embraces the boundaries as levers it can use to get to the edge.

But when you produce work that is predictably derivative, you haven't made art. You've settled for a cop-out, something safe and deniable. You can point to what came before and blame the person who made that, because, after all, all you did was make an echo.

The hard part is in taking a stand and doing it new. For the first time.

The Two Courses That Ought to Be Required of Anyone Who Wants to Make Art

Just two.

How to See

and

Finding the Guts to Make Important Work

Everything else will take care of itself.

The frustration of those who are stuck and are frustrated at not reaching their potential comes from one, the other, or both.

They don't see the world as it is, don't see the opportunities, don't see how they can help . . . or they do see it but are paralyzed with fear, unable to conquer the resistance and actually do something about it.

I'm not suggesting that you see the world as *I* see it. The way each of us sees the world is unique and there's no default view, no right answer. But if your narrative, your analysis, your reaction to the incoming world isn't giving you the insight to successfully do the work you'd like to do, it's almost certainly not the world's fault. If your view of the world leads to nothing but frustration, you've probably misdefined the safety zone, and no amount of intransigence on your part is going to change reality.

Seeing "the world as it is" is a practical tool of the successful artist. When your work doesn't resonate, when you feel as though you've missed the mark, it may be an error of interpretation. Changing the way you see and changing the assumptions you bring to the audience are the shortcuts to making better art.

Willfully Uninformed

A sad combination that I often see is someone who is giving up control by waiting to get picked, while giving in to the resistance and refusing to understand how their industry works. Without domain knowledge, without understanding the realities and points of view of all the players who are involved, the artist willingly becomes a helpless pawn.

Not only aren't you going to get picked, but it's impossible to pick yourself if you don't understand how the system works. It's far easier to whine about unfair power brokers and unethical double-dealers than it is to dive into the dynamics of how things are actually made and sold.

The unpublished author, the unsigned screenwriter, the disheartened job seeker. Sometimes these people have lost the law of large numbers. Other times, though, they are playing a game they cannot win. They don't speak the language; they are out of sync with what's being bought, with what's hot, with the needs of the audience with the power to pick them.

And if your art isn't generating the connection you seek...
Make better art.

See more accurately.

Make with more precision.

Use more guts to find your blank slate.

And if none of those works, change your venue; find a new stage to play on.

But don't question your commitment. Don't get attached to the outcome. Don't listen to the critic who universalizes his opinion.

Make better art.

You can risk being wrong or you can be boring.

What Does It Mean to Let Go of the Outcome?

How can we possibly be professionals at the same time that we don't care about what happens next?

Can we learn to accept applause without doing the work because we *expect* applause?

When you give up ownership of what you make in exchange for allowing a stranger or a critic or the masses to judge you, you have walked away from your humanity.

Worse, you corrupt the very outcome you thought you were trying to attain, because working in anticipation of the outcome actually degrades the thing you were making.

You can do your work looking in the rearview mirror, trying to re-create what has already been a success in the marketplace. This is seen as a shortcut to both getting acceptance and avoiding criticism. After all, if all you do is what's been done, how can it be your fault?

The connection economy, though, won't bother to notice the

repetitive or the boring. It won't go out of its way to engage or discuss the banal.

Almost as futile is spending all day imagining how your best work is precisely aligned with what the crowd will want in the future. The future is unknowable, and if you are betting everything on the unknowable's being in perfect connection with your idea, you will likely make nothing much. It's too hard to commit when you are relying so completely on something you can't guarantee. Again, this path leads to the ironic result that the work can't be what you're hoping for.

The artist soon sees that the only voice worth embracing is the muse. Learn your field, of course. Excel in domain knowledge. Have empathy for your customers, and care deeply about how your work will affect them. Yes, yes, and yes. But . . .

But make what you will make. Not in anticipation of or dependence on the applause of others, and not because you are totally entangled in the results. No, make it because you are committed to making it. The commitment works because you can be sure of your intent, sure of your skills, and sure of your compassion for those who will encounter what you make.

Only when you make art that isn't for everyone do you have a chance to connect with someone. And when you connect with someone, amazingly, you increase the chances that you've made something that many will want.

When It's Not Good Enough

Beat This! might be the best cookbook I've ever read. And you will have trouble finding it, because it's out of print. Terrific recipes, very funny . . . just the thing cookbook readers love. And yet it didn't sell a million copies and it hasn't been as commercially successful as it could be.

So, is it not good enough?

Artists need to think hard before they tag their work with labels like "unsuccessful" or "lousy" or even "great." Is Justin Bieber a great musician? I think it depends on what we're measuring. There's no question that if the metric is pop hits, he's far better than Jill Sobule or Dale Henderson.

The danger is in using someone else's ruler to measure your art.

If you're not achieving the results you seek, your definition of good might be wrong, or your art might not be as good as you think it is. Or you might not have gotten lucky this time around.

So learn to see even better.

Make ever better art.

And do it again.

Your Interactions Are Part of Your Art

I recently had needless surgery at the hands of a doctor who may or may not have been good with a scalpel or whatever heinous tool he used. What is certain is that after the operation was over, he destroyed his chances to create the full impact he was capable of.

Apparently, after surgery he met with me to go over the results of the procedure. Alas, he chose to do this while I was still under anesthesia, and he never bothered to call to follow up. Day after day, no contact from the doctor.

This is not so unusual among a certain generation of surgeons, as they believe that their job is to do surgery, not to actually make people get better.

A doctor's call or e-mail message can't help the patient with the physical pain, but it can provide information, solace, or just a reminder that everything is going according to plan. Does it change the surgery itself? Of course not. Does it change the outcome of that surgery? Certainly.

To the industrialist, the product is the product, the transaction is the transaction. Caveat emptor. It's yours; deal with it.

To the artist, to the human who values outcomes and connections, caring enough to call is part of the art.

When the clerk is only doing her job, or the franchisee is following the manual, or the teacher is following the union contract to the letter, they've forgone the opportunity to do art. Sure, the hotel room or the class is the product that was ostensibly paid for, but what connects people and changes them is the caring part.

This Explains Why Caring Is in Such Short Supply

The artist cares and so extends herself, creating new interactions to ensure that the recipient is changed and a connection is made....

Which means that the industrial worker is afraid to care, because to do so would mean standing up and taking responsibility for the work. It's impossible for the engaged worker to both follow instructions (which means that the boss owns the outcome) and genuinely care (which means that the clerk is responsible for what happens next).

Anyone who cares and acts on it is performing a work of art.

Steve Martin Wasn't Funny

As we saw, Martin was original, but the most successful stand-up comedian of his generation—perhaps of all time—wasn't particularly funny. Remove your cultural connection to him and listen to the work fresh, and you'll see that he wasn't a classic comedian. He was a noncomedian. He was influenced more by Sartre and Beckett than by Groucho or (Buddy) Hackett.

Martin ended his stand-up career doing sold-out arena shows to forty thousand people a night. He realized that he was the ringleader of a party, not the provider of funny. The audience brought their own funny. They loved cheering him, finishing his lines, saying his lines before he even said them.

The thing is, for ten years before he was America's most popular comedian, he was a commercial failure. It wasn't unusual for a club he was performing in to have three or four people in it. He couldn't get a record deal. He'd travel across the country to do a show in Florida, a hundred people would come, and he'd be so thrilled by the turnout it would keep him going for a month.

The act didn't change; the audience did.

The secret of Martin's work was precision. He obsessively focused on the work. Art isn't merely bold. It doesn't always involve bright colors and hysterical movements. For Martin, it might mean how he raised a hand at a certain moment or when he decided to end a bit.

He worked for a decade on being a noncomic, on determining how far he could go in a given direction. Only by honing each piece, placing it reverently in front of an audience (even three people), was he able to make it just so. Like Robert Irwin carefully finishing the back of a painting—the part that no one would ever see—Martin put his effort into the white spaces, the dead spaces, the moments in between.

And then he patiently waited for the zeitgeist to come to him.

All Artist, All the Time

This is the surprising part: People who create art are fairly normal the rest of the time—if normal means ordinary, fitting in, compliant, or even boring. Steve Jobs wore the same style and color of shirt every day so he wouldn't have to think about fashion (he owned thirty-five copies of the same turtleneck). Andy Warhol listened to the same song hundreds of times in a row to desensitize himself to audio. Speakers at the TED conference, busy making a difference in their chosen fields, sometimes have a rather dull take on food or politics or what's next.

The fact that people are artists in only one part of their lives is more proof that art isn't something you're born with. Art is an effort, an opportunity to devote enormous emotion and energy in a specific direction. It means that you care, not that you're a loner or a loon.

Because art carries risk and pain and effort along with it, it's unlikely we're going to invest in it for everything we do. The artist brings huge resources to her art, so it's naive to believe that an artist is going to be an artist everywhere and always.

The Artist as an Outsider

If you ask successful science-fiction writers to describe their childhoods, they almost always tell the same story. Parents, friends, and teachers, in general, didn't understand them. The author wasn't the most popular kid, the class president, or the homecoming queen. Perhaps there was a fabulous teacher or a special aunt who encouraged her, but generally, the author spent a lot of time on her own, sketching or writing or noticing or dreaming.

And the same stories show up when you talk to programmers, entrepreneurs, graphic artists, and others who make a ruckus. These are people who, when they were younger, could have made the choice to live a life built around fitting in. After feeling the pain of being outsiders, they could have transformed themselves into insiders.

But they didn't. The ones who make it onto our radar, the ones who have made an impact, have chosen to live a life of standing out, not fitting in. They are comfortable doing work that matters and willing to embrace the pain that the resistance causes in order to ship their work to the world.

The irony isn't lost on me. Our culture and our economy have just recently deemed these makers and shippers and ruckus makers "insiders." They have established the new society, and to be part of it, you have to be willing to stand apart from it first.

Engineering and Art

Engineering has a right answer. It is a consistent set of best practices and demonstrable proofs, repeated again and again until the answer is found.

Art has no right answer. Art can work, surely, and it can fail. Art involves the intent of the artist and the reception of the audience. And art involves an unpredictable leap.

It's possible that you have an engineering problem. If you do, go solve it.

If you have an artistic challenge, though, quit looking for the right answer.

Plenty of engineering breakthroughs begin as artistic challenges. The artist sees what hasn't been seen before or has the guts to start with a blank slate. After the artistic leap has been made, the engineers can dive in and optimize and productize the original insight. And yes, even if your job title is "engineer" or "direct-mail executive" or "letterpress operator," it's possible (and even an obligation) for you to be an artist, too.

You've Seen All of Your Shows

The only person who saw every single Jerry Garcia performance was Jerry himself. The only one who has seen every memo you've written and every meeting you've been to is you.

It's pretty easy to pick out your worst performances ever and compare them with the best your competition has ever done. Easy, but pointless.

Your best work is a gift. Of course your work can be improved, but it is a gift first. Your generosity is more important than your perfection.

The artist sees the world as it is.

The artist tells a story that resonates.

Talker's Block

No one ever gets talker's block. No one wakes up in the morning, discovers he has nothing to say, and sits quietly, for days or weeks, until the muse hits, until the moment is right, until all the craziness in his life has died down.

Why, then, is writer's block endemic?

The reason we don't get talker's block is that we're in the habit of talking without a lot of concern for whether or not our inane blather will come back to haunt us. Talk is cheap. Talk is ephemeral. Talk can be easily denied.

We talk poorly and then, eventually (or sometimes), we talk smart. We get better at talking precisely because we talk. We see what works and what doesn't and, if we're insightful, do more of what works. How can one get talker's block after all this practice?

Writer's block isn't hard to cure.

Just write. Write poorly. Continue to write poorly, in public, until you can write better.

Everyone should learn to write in public. Get a blog. Or use Squidoo or Tumblr or a microblogging site. Use an alias if you like. Turn off comments, certainly—you don't need more criticism; you need more writing.

Do it every day. Every single day. Not a diary, not fiction, but analysis. Clear, crisp, honest writing about what you see in the world. Or want to see. Or teach (in writing). Tell us how to do something.

If you know you have to write *something* every single day, even a paragraph, you will improve your writing. The resistance, of course, would rather have you write nothing, not speak up in public, keep it under wraps.

If you're concerned only with avoiding error, then not writing is not a problem, because zero is perfect and without defects. Shipping nothing is safe.

Fortunately, the second-best thing to zero is something better than bad. So if you know you have to write tomorrow, your brain will start working on something better than bad. And then you'll inevitably redefine bad and tomorrow will be better than that. And on and on.

Write like you talk. Often.

The True Measure of Your Work

The industrialist has only one measure: Did it make money?

Organize the masses. Borrow money and then spend it. Enhance productivity. Subjugate or bribe your workforce to expend more effort. Push for the win.

Did it work? Did it sell? Did you get elected? Did you raise more money for your cause? If it worked, you are successful and the pain was worth it.

The external focus of the industrialist is part of the Icarus Deception, and it corrupts how we measure ourselves, how we decide if our lives are well lived. Do I have more stuff? Is my neighborhood/car/spouse/kid as upgraded and popular as it could be?

The artist focuses on none of this. A patron or a sale or a windfall is merely a chance to make more art.

In the connection economy, the true measure of your work is whether you touched someone. The generosity and *kamiwaza* you bring to the process are part of the process, and the ability to detach from the outcome permits you to bring more of them.

"What did you do and why did you do it?" These questions matter more than "Did the critics like it?"

The industrialists sold us on a stepwise road to success, with tickets punched along the way and obvious external measures of progress, from grades to paychecks to job titles.

The artist gives up the benefit of these dancing-monkey treats and receives in exchange the peace of mind from work well done.

The World's Worst Boss

That would be you.

Even if you're not self-employed, your boss is you. You manage your career, your day, your responses. You manage how you sell your services and your education and the way you talk to yourself.

Odds are, you're doing it poorly.

If you had a manager who talked to you the way you talked to you, you'd quit. If you had a boss who wasted as much of your time as you do, she'd be fired. If an organization developed its employees as poorly as you are developing yourself, it would soon go under.

I'm amazed at how often people choose to fail when they go out on their own or when they end up in one of those rare jobs that encourages them to set an agenda and manage themselves. Faced with the freedom to excel, they falter and hesitate and stall and ultimately punt.

We are surprised when someone self-directed arrives on the scene. Someone who figures out a way to work from home and then turns that into a two-year journey, laptop in hand, as he explores the world while doing his job. We are shocked that someone uses evenings and weekends to get a second education or start a useful new side business. And we're envious when we encounter someone who has managed to bootstrap herself into happiness, as if that were rare or even uncalled for.

Before you had the world's worst boss, it's likely you were the world's worst teacher. We can't rely on others to be our teachers anymore, particularly after we turn ten. No, the future belongs to individuals who decide to become great bosses (and teachers).

Unsafe Working Conditions

If you work for the world's worst boss, you have no one to blame but yourself.

We'd have no sympathy for the marathon runner who lost every race because she refused to train or stretch.

We'd never visit a doctor who wouldn't go to continuing education courses or read the journals.

And yet it's easy to spend your day at a job hiding from the real work, the stuff you actually get paid to accomplish. Easier to blame it on writer's block or on not being in the right frame of mind or on needing to keep up with Twitter.

If your work is to do art, then doing art is what you ought to be organizing your energy and your time around. Excuses aren't welcome; the work (your work) that connects is all we are seeking.

Hire Yourself

If you work on your own or in a small, fast-moving company or even at a place with a lick of sense, you'll discover that you have the ability to hire a version of yourself. To find someone who does every checklist task you do, probably better than you do it. Take the part of your job you can describe in a manual, and hire someone to do it.

Why would you do that?

Because then you'd be that new hire's boss.

The scary thing about doing this is that you'd have to find something to do, because you can't do what you used to (you just hired someone to do that). You'd be on the hook not only to find something to do but to do it so well that it more than paid for the person you just hired to do your old job.

You'd have to do more art.

You'd have to spend all your time not just imagining a bigger, better future but also making it happen. If you didn't have to spend your time in meetings and reacting to incoming, no one would be standing in the way of your ability to generate value and insight and forward motion.

The people with more leverage than you don't work any harder than you do. They've hired people to do that. No, the people with more leverage than you do are making better art.

Hire Your Boss

The alternative to hiring someone to do what you do is to hire someone whom you can work for. Entrepreneurs often do this when they raise money from venture capitalists. The VCs end up on the board; they are the ones who demand quarterly results and who scour spreadsheets and corporate-strategy decks and then give their permission.

Painters do this when they sign on with a gallery instead of selling their work directly to the public. Musicians do it when they give away all their rights to a record label (for some much-needed cash) instead of scrounging to control everything.

If your art involves the texture of creation, the nitty-gritty of making and shipping, then by all means, this is a great strategy. The trade-off is that you will give up much of your freedom, particularly the freedom to decide what sort of art you're going to make.

Turning Your Art into a Job

Our cultural instincts die hard. Frequently, people who succeed with a breakthrough or the creation of connection then work hard to ensure that they never have to do it again.

They turn one original restaurant into a chain of a hundred restaurants, ensuring that the insight and innovation will never have to be repeated and all the founder will have to do going forward is go to meetings.

Our fear of having to do it again, combined with the industrialist's ability to reliably churn out cash on demand, means that we sign up for sequels, structure, and systems. Instead of aggressively pursuing the freedom to succeed or fail with the next thing, we sign up to sing the same pop song every night, to use the same boilerplate contract next time, and to be sure that version 2.0 is a lot like version 1.0.

You don't have to sign away your art to make things happen. Acknowledge that making art is unpredictable, bumpy, and sometimes painful, but do it anyway. The less job you have to do, the more likely it is you'll find the guts to make art.

Turning Your Job into Art

On the other hand, anyone with a job has the privilege of turning that job's tasks into art of one kind or another. If you transform your job into a platform for art, you're leveraging the trust and education and smarts you were given and putting them to good use.

No, you can't walk into your boss's office and demand a clean sheet of paper and unlimited time and authority. What you can do is take responsibility. You can make small connections, small experiments, and small failures and own the results. You can honestly and clearly report what you're learning and what you're making and then do it again.

Most of the day is spent in little work, doing your job. Clerical tasks, bureaucratic stuff, meetings, polishing, improving, reacting, responding.

The obligation is to carve out time for the big work, the work of art. The big work that scares you, that brings risk, that might very well fail.

And we're most likely to do that work when it's least expected, when the table is small, the resources are lacking, and time is short.

No need to wait for permission or the lightning bolt of inspiration. The big work is available to you as soon as you decide to do it.

You don't get to do your big work at the big table right away, though. You get to do it at the little table first, without resources and without authority. And then, if you persist, over time you'll find you can spend more of your time at your job doing your work, which is your art. And if your current gig doesn't appreciate you, someone else will.

Evil Olive: Blowing Up the Boundaries

One misperception about art is that it abhors boundaries. Art to some people means operating without rules, with full freedom and with no consequences.

This is silly. Without boundaries, you can't make art. Art lives on the edge of the boundaries.

Palindromes, for example, require writing a sentence that's the same forward and backward. Something like: "No, Mel Gibson is a casino's big lemon."

If you pushed to do palindromes that didn't actually reflect letter by letter, that would certainly change the status quo, but I'm not sure they'd be worth much. It's too easy to make defective palindromes.

Yes, I know you can make a good movie for twenty million dollars, but all we have is five. Yes, I know that your retail store would do better if you were on Main Street, but there's no room there; there's room here. And yes, I know it would be better if you had more time, but no, we don't.

Pick which rules to break, and embrace the rest.

Artists Don't Want to Go to Meetings

Jason Fox says, "The art of compromise is knowing when not to." To put it another way, "It's best to get as many people as possible into one room. And then go somewhere else."

The meeting is a temporary collection of people waiting for someone to take responsibility so everyone else can go back to work. If you want someone else to take the blame and give you the credit, you will wait a very long time.

The Juilliard Dilemma

To give you an idea of how hard-core the Juilliard School in New York is, when a world-class violinist recently gave a speech and performance, only fifteen students came, but every single practice room was booked solid.

Students here have more desire to practice the notes as written than they have to be coached by a master.

That's because what got them into school was their ability to do the job of playing the music as written. What led to their acceptance to this famous institution was their skill in playing the notes, combined with a willingness to carefully follow instructions.

The dilemma is this: What got them in isn't going to do them any good at all when they leave.

The world doesn't have a shortage of very good violin players. There is no scarcity of obedient tympani players at established orchestras. They're not hiring for these positions, and even if they were, supply far exceeds demand.

No, the only thing that will sustain these extraordinarily talented students going forward is going to be original art. Playing music in ways that no one expects. That's a leap that they've been culturally encouraged to avoid.

Three Insights of the Impresario

1. If you weren't born with talent, that's fine. You were born with commitment.
2. Organize the talented.
3. Connect the disconnected.

From "What Can I Get" to "What Can I Give"

In the industrial economy, the game is zero sum. Every productive action generates a reward, and that reward belongs either to management or to labor. There's an inherent conflict here because scarce resources must be divided.

In the connection economy, on the other hand, connections create surplus. With so many choices, much of what was scarce is now abundant.

The challenge, then, is to reorient for a world of abundance—specifically, to focus on figuring out how you can add to the network before worrying about what you can take from it. If you add enough, the taking will take care of itself.

Of Course We Need Industrial Work Done

Of course we need to have coal mined, molecules moved, pages printed, and documents sorted.

But that doesn't mean that *you* have to do it. The power is shifting, fast, from those who provide things that are no longer scarce to those who invent art that leads to connection. The industrial economy won't disappear, but the agenda will increasingly be set by those who make connection, not widgets.

We Get Better at What We Practice

So what are you practicing?

—barely making deadlines
—skeptically shooting down new ideas
—being generous
—doing art
—grumbling
—looking for opportunities

—dreaming pipe dreams

—giving useful feedback

On Good Taste

Ira Glass understands how you feel:

> Nobody tells this to people who are beginners, I wish someone told me. All of us who do creative work, we get into it because we have good taste. But there is this gap. For the first couple years you make stuff, it's just not that good. It's trying to be good, it has potential, but it's not. But your taste, the thing that got you into the game, is still killer. And your taste is why your work disappoints you. A lot of people never get past this phase, they quit. Most people I know who do interesting, creative work went through years of this. We know our work doesn't have this special thing that we want it to have. . . . And if you are just starting out or you are still in this phase, you gotta know it's normal and the most important thing you can do is do a lot of work. . . . It is only by going through a volume of work that you will close that gap, and your work will be as good as your ambitions.

Risky Rice

All mediocre sushi bars use electric rice cookers. They are reliable, foolproof, cheap, and easy. And they make perfectly good rice.

Extraordinary sushi bars, the ones that cost two or three times as much as the average ones, never use electric rice cookers. They use gas. And a timer.

The thing is, the gas is uneven and a little unpredictable. It's much harder to make good rice in a gas rice cooker. It takes time and attention and talent.

But only with a flame is it possible to make *great* rice. It's unlikely that you'll create something scarce without doing something risky to get there.

Become a Patron of the Arts

It's interesting that the phrase we use isn't "a patron of the art." We mean the arts, plural. You don't have to like this project or that act or this piece. What a patron does is respect the artist, the commitment to the path of making a difference. Your opinion about a particular employee's new idea is not nearly as important as how you act in the face of the things he does that don't work or might not work.

Only industrialists in love with the status quo can insist on everything working every time. For the rest of us, the best path is to become a patron and to surround ourselves with people willing to do the undone and to take responsibility for what happens next.

when man determined to destroy

himself he picked the was

of shall and finding only why

smashed it into because.

—E. E. Cummings

When the Audience Meets the Art

Marcel Duchamp pointed out, "It is the observer who makes the painting." Duchamp created a stage and let the viewer act out the art in her mind.

But Yves Klein said, "My paintings are only the ashes of my art." For him, the creation of the work was the art, and the canvas or the photo or the fake newspaper was merely the souvenir.

They're both getting at the same truth: The artist leaps, and the viewer experiences the power of that leap. To leap in the dark, to be the silent tree falling in the forest where no one can hear it—that's insufficient.

For the leap to matter, others have to experience it. It must come with the possibility of rejection or ennui or epic failure. And it must come with the gift of allowing the audience to experience some of the mythic, human elation of leaping as well.

The Experience of the Novice

What if the viewer doesn't know the backstory? What if the restaurant patron doesn't understand how difficult molecular gastronomy is? What if the tourist at MoMA knows nothing of the history of art and doesn't realize what an astonishing risk Jackson Pollock took?

Pollock's teacher, Thomas Hart Benton, was a skilled painter, creating figures that were almost sculptural in their dimensionality. To go from this informed realism to drip paintings . . .

Of course, to novices, the leap isn't evident. "Anyone can do this," they might think. They don't understand that the art isn't merely what Pollock put on the canvas; in some ways, the canvas is just the ashes of his art.

And this is why art is rarely for the masses. The masses don't appreciate the flash of originality and are happy to buy the copy or the knockoff. But that's fine, because the masses matter less than they ever did before. The masses are interested in what's popular, and the weird, the ones who get the joke, have more influence than ever in bringing ideas to them.

We're all the masses sometime. We're part of the masses when we don't appreciate nuance, when we merely want what is good enough, when price matters more than impact. The explosion of niches, of diverse tastes amplified, of weirdness, means that the masses are easier to ignore now.

The artist may choose her audience. And if you choose an audience that understands the work, it opens the door to pushing the work even further.

The Simple Reason That Creativity, Leadership, and Brainstorming Books and Courses Fail . . .

. . . is that people don't *want* them to work. We've been brainwashed into becoming afraid of art.

It's not hard to learn to dig a ditch if you believe that digging a ditch is going to pay off.

People hesitate to lead or to invent or to make art because they're afraid of what will happen if they do.

There are no step-by-step instructions or shortcuts in this book because those are easy to find elsewhere. I will, though, share two simple tactics that will expose your fear for what it is and let you look it straight in the eye.

Tactic: Problem and Solution Cards

At a recent event, I handed out stacks of beautiful hand-printed index cards. One side was labeled PROBLEM and the other said SOLUTION.

I asked everyone to write down their real problem, their cherished roadblock, the thing that was holding them back and keeping them from making their art. It might be the ten thousand dollars they needed to finish funding the project, or the annoying boss who wouldn't say yes, or the fact that they couldn't get an audition with a major label. What was that perfect problem, the one they just couldn't solve?

And then I asked everyone to swap cards with the person sitting next to them. I gave everyone five minutes to do their best and write down a solution on the back of the card.

Here's the thing: I didn't really care if the solution was any good. Instead, I cared about three things:

First, how did it feel to write down the problem? The act of making it concrete, of writing it down and sharing it—did it make the problem seem bigger, or, more likely, did it trivialize this mammoth problem that you'd been polishing and cherishing and carrying around, maybe for years?

Second, how did it feel to know that the person sitting next to you was maybe, just maybe, going to write down a valid solution? Because if she did, you'd have to act on it, wouldn't you? You wouldn't have your problem anymore, your bluff would be called, and you'd actually have to take action and ship your art. You'd find out once and for all if the audience was going to embrace your project, ignore it, or call you out as a fraud.

And third, if the person sitting next to you failed to solve your problem adequately (which was likely, since everyone had only five minutes), were you prepared to admit that the problem was unsolvable? Because an unsolvable problem is almost as good as a solved one. An unsolvable problem means that you can declare defeat and move on. It means you can eliminate this excuse from your almanac of excuses, because your goal is unrealistic. No, I will never be able to become invisible or fly or even sing opera. But I accept these limits, and I've lived my life around them. Life without a bag filled with unsolved problems is a lot lighter, and you can get a lot more done.

All art is wonder-ful. Until the project works, the audience will wonder if the artist is merely reckless.

Tactic: The Focus Group

Not that kind of focus group. This is a group loosely based on the classic Mastermind idea created by Napoleon Hill. Find exactly three other artists—who work in different fields, who come from different backgrounds, who pursue different goals—and connect with one another about the process of your art.

The object of this group isn't to help you see better or make better art. The object is to remind you of your commitment and to push you to make your art more original, personal, and successful.

When you know that you need to meet every two weeks and look a respected artist in the eye and tell her what you did (or didn't) make, it will raise your game.

Do What You Want

Those are the most frightening four words brought to us by the connection revolution.

If you want to sing, sing. If you want to lead, lead. If you want to touch, connect, describe, disrupt, give, support, build, question . . . do it. You will not be picked. But if you want to pick yourself, go for it.

The cost is that you own the results.

The Worst-Case-Scenario Generator

Writer Nicholas Bate points out that evolution has endowed us with a very useful but now mostly obsolete tool. Our lizard brain is quick to imagine the worst-case scenario for every one of our artistic actions.

If your WCSG is busy telling you that the toaster is going to start a fire or the car will explode, then you're probably not functioning in a useful way. Ordinary objects in the course of an ordinary day carry little danger. We reserve the imaginary WCSG device for the art in our lives, for the new, for projects that matter. It tells us to crawl at precisely the moments we ought to be leaping.

For most of us, the worst-case scenarios are not just unrealistic; they are debilitating. We imagine the worst possible outcome of giving a speech or writing a memo or launching a new product. The very things that ought to be at the center of our optimism are often seen as threats and risks.

Amazingly, none of those disasters has ever occurred. Yet the generator persists, amplifying the downsides in a counterproductive effort to keep us safe. The problem, of course, is that our comfort zone is no longer aligned with the safety zone.

We think we're being safe and smart and conservative and avoiding flying too close to the sun. But all the generator is doing is pushing us closer and closer to the waves, so that we're flying too low, daring too little, and blowing our best chance ever to matter.

"I Never Thought You'd Amount to Anything"

A challenge the artist faces is that the work is going to be seen, and it is *your* work.

As an artist, you realize that this work is not the assignment of another, not the fill-in-the-blank, paint-by-numbers iteration of someone else's work, but yours.

Your work.

And if it doesn't resonate, that rejection feels personal.

And if it *does* resonate, you own that, too.

It's so much easier to live a life in the shadows, where you never have to deal with either impostor syndrome or rejection. You never have to confront the fraudulent feeling of being called talented or the horror of being recognized as a fraud. So much easier to hide.

Success can be just as fraught with danger as failure, because it opens more doors and carries more responsibility.

The alternative, though, is to be invisible and to deny your dreams. How can we even contemplate this?

Given the choice, we have no choice. We have to create, and to own it.

You're a Fraud and You Know It

That's at the heart of the artist's fear of shame. Deep down, we're worried that we will be discovered as the frauds that we know we are.

You're not typing at eighty-nine words per minute or mixing together the same chemicals you mixed yesterday. You are daring to fly close to the sun. You are doing the new thing, the thing no one has ever dared to do before. You are saying what hasn't been said, touching what hasn't been touched. Of course you are a fraud. What could possibly qualify you to do this?

If you don't stand out, you'll never need to stand up. And no one will call you on what you say or what you do or what you believe. You're back in your comfort zone, but as we've seen, there's no safety left there.

Everyone is lonely and everyone feels like a fraud. I feel like a fraud as I type this, as I brush my teeth, and every time I go on-stage.

This is part of the human condition. Accepted. Now what?

Complaining is stupid. Either act or forget.

—Stefan Sagmeister

Jante's Law

About a hundred years ago, Scandinavian author Aksel Sandemose wrote a book about the culture of his hometown, Nykøbing Mors, a place where conforming to the norm is essential and no one is anonymous. He described ten rules (which he named after a character in the book, Jante) that are still acted on and taught in many cultures and many schools:

Don't think you're anything special.
Don't think you're as good as we are.

Don't think you're smarter than we are.

Don't convince yourself that you're better than we are.

Don't think you know more than we do.

Don't think you are more important than we are.

Don't think you are good at anything.

Don't laugh at us.

Don't think anyone cares about you.

Don't think you can teach us anything.

And the bonus rule, which brings shame and vulnerability to the forefront:

Don't think that there aren't a few things we know about you.

This indoctrination is how you destroy any hope that art will happen. This is what the industrialist believes, and he used to be right. But no longer.

"Agility Beats Tactics"

Joi Ito, head of MIT's Media Lab, has a problem with the myth of Hernán Cortés.

In the story, Cortés orders his soldiers to "burn those boats." If there's no turning back, the theory goes, then the army will fight harder because they know they have no alternative.

But there is always an alternative.

In the idea-driven connection economy, the cost of experiments is lower than ever, the ability to coordinate is high, and the impact of being right is huge.

As a result, we're not going to reward massively organized

efforts that require the burning of boats. Instead, the simple idea that captures the imagination of a few and then spreads is certain to dominate.

Please understand a key distinction: It makes sense to be agile with your tactics, with your approach, with the way you seek to make an impact. But please don't question your standing as an artist.

Art is the only strategy available, and we must defend our right and our willingness to do art regardless of who is criticizing us and regardless of what market failure we face.

Yes, change your tactics, and often. Agility pays. But no, don't give up your strategy of making art.

The Reason They (We) Need You

There is work that you (and only you) can do.

You can be the essential linchpin in the process, and we desperately need you to step up and offer us that work.

That's the best kind of art. The art only you are capable of.

In the words of FDR, "That is no vision of a distant millennium. It is a definite basis for a kind of world attainable in our own time and generation." A world attainable is around the corner if we conquer the negative chatter that subverts our art.

Worth Noting

They will tell you that it's easy (it's not).

They will tell you that it's fun (it is, but only sometimes).

They will tell you that you must be born with it (not true).

And they will tell you that it's not your turn (and they are wrong).

Who Gets the Blues?

"I've got the blues."

"I have a wart on my foot."

"I have a cold."

"I have a broken arm."

Isn't it interesting that we never say, "I am a broken arm" or "I am cancer"? We understand that these are things that happen *to* us; they are not who we are.

And yet we say, "I am afraid," and "I am a failure." Of course, afraid isn't who we are; afraid is something that happened to us. Failure is an event, not a person.

The only thing that's clearly true is this: "You are an artist."

You Are Not Your Art

When the criticism rolls in, when the project is turned down, or when your sales call is rejected, it's easy (automatic, human, likely) to assume that you have been rejected.

After all, when the project is embraced, it feels as though you're being embraced—and so rejection must mean precisely the flip side, that they hate you because they hate your work.

But that's artistic suicide.

It's not useful to put yourself on the line, life or death, do or die. You are an artist, not the art. The only way to be vulnerable and go to the edge is to realize that if your art doesn't work, you'll be back tomorrow with more (better) art.

The Hobgoblin

The mythical Steve Jobs is often celebrated for his taste. He had, it's said, an unerring ability to see quality, to understand what the right answer was, to consistently cleave any problem to find the one best answer.

Except this isn't at all true.

Tim Cook, Apple's CEO, recently said, "He would flip on something so fast that you would forget that he was the one taking the 180-degree polar [opposite] position the day before."

The magic of Steve Jobs wasn't in being right. It was in being sure.

The Freedom from Pain Comes by Embracing the Pain

The pain-free life will elude you. You can work to smooth out all the edges, to eliminate all risk, and to be sure that everyone you encounter likes you. (I hope that seeing this in writing helps you see the absurdity of that mission.)

But in the unlikely event that you accomplish this, you'll soon be beset by the knowledge that it won't last long and that it's only a matter of time before someone comes along and ruins the entire thing. When a performer tries to keep a room of a thousand people still and quiet, it takes only one heckler to break the silence.

The alternative is to not only accept but embrace the fact that your work (your best work) will bring you the joy of creation juxtaposed with the shouting of the lizard brain.

Once you acknowledge that this pain is both a signal and a marker, you don't have to waste energy in organizing your life to make the pain go away. In fact, you can play a different game instead—figuring out how much you can stand. It's the pain (and the fear of pain) that makes art scarce. If it were merely fun (and it can be fun!), then there'd be too much of it, and it wouldn't be worth much.

Now you have the foundation for true freedom, because you are no longer limiting your passion and your art in search of an absence of fear. Now that fear is part of your work, you can ignore it and work as if you were fearless.

Freedom isn't the ability to do whatever you want. It's the willingness to do whatever you want.

The Leverage of Limits

In a capitalist system, corporations are organized around creating more. More profit, more market share, more power. And the organization will always want the shortest, fastest, most reliable route to more.

And so the corporation dumps chemicals in the river because it's not against the law. The nonprofit raises money from the same donors again and again because it's easier than finding new donors. The marketer spams a mailing list again and again because it's easier than treasuring the attention of the audience for the long haul.

Organizations that are competing in a breakneck race to the bottom (lower prices, lower quality, less art) will sometimes get there, which does no one any good.

Consider the oligopolistic carbonated-beverage industry. The easiest way for these companies to grow was to target the under-educated and poorest segment of the market, pushing ever-larger drink sizes on them. "Share of stomach" was the name for their strategy—not to increase market share alone or profit alone but to control every ounce of liquid consumed.

When Mike Bloomberg, mayor of New York, ordered the size of a cup of sugared soda limited to sixteen ounces (which was, according to Coca-Cola's advertising fifty years ago, a serving suitable for *three* people), the industry went ballistic. They acted as though this were an unconscionable limit on their free-market right to sell as much as they could, even if it made their customers sick.

They're missing a key truth: If the limit applies to them and to their competition, that limit will require them to compete on insight and creativity and innovation, not on racing to sell the maximum volume. The limit will also increase the life span of their customers, which is probably a good thing.

Every artist needs to wrestle with establishing limits, because without them, there's no opportunity for leverage, for finding a new way to solve an old problem. So the play has to take place in this sort of theater, and the device has to cost less than forty-five dollars, and the surface temperature can't exceed eighty-three degrees.

Yes, artists break limiting rules all the time, but when they do, they do it selectively and they do it on purpose.

Mono No Aware

Your art won't last. And sometimes the most beautiful and important things are the ones we see fading away. Japanese scholar Motoori Norinaga coined the term *mono no aware* to describe the feeling we get when we see cherry blossoms wither and die, when we interact with a thing that's important or beautiful and know that it is going away. It's sort of a reverse nostalgia.

It's not that different from the essential concept of *memento mori*, a Latin term that reminds us that we're all going to die.

Understanding impermanence is the twin sister of understanding art. All art, as we've seen, brings something new into the world, but that newness can't remain, or there would be no room for more art. Newness fades.

The impermanence of art (and the impermanence of us, the creators of art) isn't a bad thing, any more than the tail of a coin is a bad thing when you're hoping for heads. You can't have one without the other.

The man who invented the ship invented the shipwreck. The creation of art also means the fading of art, and the realization that the act of making it last forever is also the act of destroying what made it work in the first place.

Dancing on the Edge of Finished

Before, when your shift was done, you were finished. When the in-box was empty, when the forms were processed, you could stop.

Now, of course, there's always one more tweet to make, one more post to write, one more Words with Friends move to complete. There's one more e-mail message you can write, one more lens you can construct, one more comment you can respond to. If you want to, you can be never finished.

And that's the dance. Facing a sea of infinity, it's easy to despair, sure that you will never reach dry land, never have the sense of accomplishment of saying, "I'm done." At the same time, to be finished, done, complete—this is a bit like being dead. The silence and the feeling that maybe that's all.

For the marketer, the freelancer, and the entrepreneur, the challenge is to reset your comfort level, to be okay with the undone, with the cycle of never ending.

We were trained to finish our homework, our peas, and our chores. Today we're never finished, and that's okay.

It's a dance, not a grind.

Dancing on the Edge of Ridiculous

All important work is ridiculous until it makes an impact, and then it becomes art.

Too ridiculous, though, and no impact is made. Not ridiculous—not important.

The hard part of bringing art to your tribe, your culture, or your market is understanding where the line between boring and ridiculous lies. Just as the dancer doesn't get it right each time, you'll take a while to triangulate, to hit and miss and then miss again until you figure out where the sweet spot lies. The dancer misses but keeps dancing, over and over until he gets it right. The same is true for the artist.

See, then make, then reinvent on the blank slate. And repeat until you've accomplished the connection you seek.

Spectators

The gods are not spectators. Consumers are spectators. The fans in the stands are spectators.

Marketers like spectators because guessing what they will do is easy and safe. You can build budgets and projections around spectators.

The publish-first-publish-often magic of the Internet punishes the spectator. The YouTube video maker gets more out of making a video than you get out of watching it. The entrepreneur and the poet and the writer each benefit from making their points, and they need readers and listeners and customers and spectators.

Sure, we'll always need spectators. But they don't have to be you.

What Do You Think?

"I'm just here to listen."

"I don't have enough experience to have an opinion."

"I'm taking notes."

"Will this be on the exam?"

Really? You came to the meeting, to the class, to the concert and you refuse to think? Or to share what you're thinking?

To reverse Descartes: You are. So think.

Speak up.

The resistance is evolution's way to keep us from making art.

Is the Artist Free?

Free to choose, free to switch, free to make whatever ruckus she chooses, sure.

But not free of the lizard brain. Not free of the voice of insecurity or second thoughts. Ever.

If you have decided that you can't do art until you quiet the voice of the resistance, *you will never do art*. Art is the act of doing work that matters while dancing with the voice in your head that screams for you to stop. We can befriend the lizard, lull it into a stupor, or merely face it down, but it's there, always.

As soon as you embrace the lizard (not merely tolerate it but engage it as a partner in your art), then you are free.

Habits of Successful Artists

The professional artist can set the table, establish a baseline, and develop habits that will serve him well when the lizard is particularly wild, when the resistance will do anything at all to stop the work.

Here are a few:

Learn to sell what you've made.
Say thank you in writing.
Speak in public.
Fail often.
See the world as it is.
Make predictions.
Teach others.
Write daily.
Connect others.
Lead a tribe.

If you commit to this basket (or another basket that matches your vision) and you make *this* your job, make *this* the task set you are accountable for, then the art you produce may very well take care of itself.

On the other hand, if your habits are reactions and responses, if they involve processing the incoming, going to meetings, and acting on the instructions of others, you have given in to the resistance; you have sacrificed your art to the whims of others.

That's wrong. That's brilliant. That's stupid. That's amazing.

Do you hear this often enough?
Don't avoid the work that creates gasps.

Hooked on a Metaphor

You probably have enough. You probably want more.

I'm not sure more of what. More feedback or more money or more acolytes. More power or more freedom or more respect.

The essential decision you'll need to make is this: Do you really want more of that, or is the thing you're measuring merely a metaphor or a stand-in for something else, something more real?

Figure out what the real thing is and don't get distracted by the easy-to-measure scorekeeping placeholders.

Making art hurts.

But it's better than the alternative.

The Poundstone Shift

Comedian Paula Poundstone didn't always play to packed houses. Like all comedians on their way up, she often found herself standing, in the middle of the night, in a practically deserted club.

In describing how she dealt with the tiny houses (two or three people in the audience!), she describes how she shifted from being angry at the crowd to being grateful—hey, these guys were the ones who came!

Your art exists to connect. At first the connections will be scarce, and it's easy to get frustrated. Is this all there is? After all this work, after all this risk, just a few people are reading or listening or bothering to show up?

The Poundstone shift reminds us that those who show up are the good guys, the ones to treasure.

"The rest of the world" isn't nearly as important as the few who are here.

"She Lets Her Clients Water Down Her Work"

My colleague and I were reviewing the portfolio of a designer, and it became clear that her work was good, but hardly great.

Then it occurred to us that we were seeing her published work, and with a little bit of reading between the lines, it was possible to see hints of greatness there.

The designer had made two mistakes. First, in a misguided attempt to get her work out there, she had let clients who weren't as good as she is go ahead and dumb down her work. Second, she hadn't widely shown her unpublished work, the kind of stuff that would attract the sort of clients that she probably deserves.

And we can learn two things from this. The first is that every time you work with someone who makes your work less than it ought to be, you've made a choice and you'll need to live with the consequences. It's also worth noting how cheap it is to build a portfolio of just about any sort of work now, and you hide your most daring work at your own peril.

Box 5

A motivated friend used Google Docs to make a four-entry questionnaire. Each box on the form asked about different elements of her strengths. She sent the form to her friends and asked them to anonymously fill it out. A perfect way to get the straight scoop about what she was good at and ought to focus on.

Unfortunately, she was missing box 5.

Box 5 was the question "What am I afraid of?"

"What am I hiding from? What is holding me back from offering my best work?"

And the answer (for most of us, most of the time) is that we're being held back by fear. The fear of being seen as a fraud.

A talented executive coach can change your life. A coach can certainly pay for herself in no time. And yet few of the people who would benefit end up hiring one. Why? Because it involves asking about box 5. We don't want to put ourselves at risk of being seen as arrogant or acting with hubris, because the shame of being seen as a fraud lurks right around the corner.

If you knew what you were afraid of, if you understood where your art lies and how fearful you are to let it out, would you take action? Or is the risk just too high?

Bill Murray on Improv . . .

You've gotta go out there and improvise and you've gotta be completely unafraid to die. You've got to be able to take a chance to die. And you have to die lots. You have to die all the time. You're goin' out there with just a whisper of an idea. The fear will make you clench up. That's the fear of dying. When you start and the first few lines don't grab and people are going like, "What's this? I'm not laughing and I'm not interested," then you just put your arms out like this and open way up and that allows your stuff to go out. Otherwise it's just stuck inside you.

The essential lesson from Bill's riff is that you're not going to die. Not really. It only feels that way.

The resistance will manufacture whatever emotions it can to persuade you to avoid dying, or anything that feels like dying.

It's pointless to deny these emotions, but you can embrace them.

When There Is No Right Answer

. . . then anything you do is open to criticism.

Here's a pile of alphabet blocks. Build something.

This is astonishingly difficult for some people. "Astonishing" is a bad word choice, actually, because the reason it's difficult is obvious: We taught you to avoid situations like this.

To be in this situation is to be vulnerable. You might build the wrong thing, a dumb thing, a trivial thing. You might spell out a phrase that offends or build a tower that's banal.

Easier to phone it in, to dismiss the exercise as childish, to do the safe and easy and defensible alternative.

A problem is a chance for you to do your best.

—Duke Ellington

And the connection economy creates nothing but problems.

The only way to get good at solving problems is to solve them. Not in private, not in a safe way, not in a place where you can waffle about the results. In public.

Scarcity and the Search for Safe

Grace Yvonne Attard writes, "I find that whenever I come from a place of scarcity and lack of faith, i.e., safe, the results of my choices always have me playing small. Choosing to lead, from the heart, from a place of serving and abundance . . . that's almost always better."

Scarcity is the dominant driver of the industrial age. Scarce resources, scarce machines, scarce labor, and scarce shelf space. The connection economy thrives on abundance. Connection creates more connection. Trust creates more trust. Ideas create more ideas.

Grace's point about faith is intricately connected to scarcity and safety. When you're doing what you've done before, all that's required is a slight belief in the laws of physics. On the other hand, to leap into the void without a map invites failure and terror and, yes, brilliance.

Columbus's Egg

Chasing is so easy.

As soon as you see something done, the lizard brain relaxes. It knows it can be done and doesn't fret so much about dying.

And so we chase ideas. We chase market leaders. We chase the next big thing down the road.

The Internet brings those things to our doorstep. We can instantly see what's (apparently) worth chasing now.

The apocryphal story about Columbus is that after he returned from a voyage, the naysayers in the elite were giving him a hard time about his trip, pointing out that if he hadn't done it, well, someone else would have done it anyway. It was inevitable, no big deal. According to a book written in 1565, this is how he dealt with his critics:

> Columbus did not respond to these words but asked for a whole egg to be brought to him. He placed it on the table and said: "My lords, I will lay a wager with any of you that you are unable to make this egg stand on its end like I will do without any kind of help or aid." They all tried without success and when the egg returned to Columbus, he tapped it gently on the table breaking it slightly and, with this, the egg stood on its end. All those present were confounded and understood what he meant: that once the feat has been done, anyone knows how to do it.

Quit chasing. It's easy, it's ineffective, and you're better than that.

Find your own egg.

The Artist's Balance:
Making Good Enough Art

The lizard brain is a wily beast, and it will go to extraordinary lengths to hide.

It will start by denying its existence, poking holes in the arguments for making art. It will make you sleepy or distract you with some other more urgent task. It will sabotage your work so that no one sees it, so you won't be asked to do it again. The resistance will slow you or stop you or make you miserable if it believes that it can get you to hide again.

One of the lizard's most pernicious tactics is to push you to fall in love with the impossible project, with the impossible dream, with the worthy but ultimately doomed mission.

After all, if your quest is one that can't possibly be achieved, how can anyone blame you for not achieving it?

Making change is difficult, and it requires the artist to lean in, to violate norms, to persist against the status quo. Sometimes that makes you a leader and an agent of change, and sometimes it makes you an annoying gadfly.

Is there a substantive difference? Isn't this just history calling the winners one thing and the losers another? Was Dennis Kucinich a crank while Daniel Ellsberg was a prescient hero?

I think there's more to it than merely the judgment after the fact. It comes back to *prajna*, to the ability to see the world as it is. By all means, we need people who will tilt at windmills, but the essence of Don Quixote was that, at some level, he *knew* they were windmills. The fearless agent of change isn't waiting for a miracle; she's building alliances and gaining stepwise support in an orderly approach to making the change she seeks. The artist on a mission makes progress, converts a few, and builds a tribe. The gadfly, on the other hand, is in love with his role as an underdog who is not responsible for much and in fact shies away from the compromises that would ultimately lead to real impact.

Three Ways to Engage with the Audience

Some artists willfully ignore their audience. "Here it is; it's done; you're dead to me." The take-it-or-leave-it attitude takes guts, but it ensures that you'll be making art without distraction. This is the art of Thomas Pynchon, David Mamet, and Trevanian. In order to live productively with the lizard brain, this artist chooses to isolate himself.

Some artists understand that they will please only their tribe—those who are looking for the response that these artists are seeking to evoke, those who share a worldview. These artists consider the art deficient until they've created something that resonates with this group, and they will care enough and engage enough to connect with the audience until the art begins to work. Bob Dylan and Cindy Sherman and David Sedaris live in this world. They're present, but they're not interested at all in pandering to the audience that doesn't get their work.

And some (I won't call them artists) will eagerly listen to every criticism and work to water down the art to pander to the largest possible audience. For this person, market share means more than art does. And so we see old Elvis become a Las Vegas parody and old Judy Garland hit bottom onstage. They started as artists intent on changing the status quo for a tribe who cared but grew into mass-market entertainers instead.

The Good Fail: How Does the Organization Get Boring?

David Puttnam, exiled Hollywood chieftain, is credited with this law: "It is more acceptable to fail in conventional ways than in unconventional ways. And its corollary: The reward for succeeding in unconventional ways is less than the risk of failing in unconventional ways. In short, you can screw up with impunity so long as you screw up like everybody else."

When we talk about failure to those raised in the industrial age, they have trouble finding artistic ways to think about it. They understand the common failure, the acceptable failure, the easy failure because that's the failure that has been done before, and they believe that this is the failure that's being requested.

But boring is the result.

This is the failure of a new flavor of Domino's pizza or a new variation of a Dell computer or the tepid reaction to the latest Corvette. They are boring failures because there wasn't much risk in the first place.

Remarkable comes from being able to risk an entirely new kind of failure, the failure that comes with a new risk. When you take the new risk, you open the door to an entirely new form of success.

I don't believe in much, but I do believe in you.

The Game Is Infinite if You Play It That Way

If it's work, the instinct is to do less of it. Why ask for more?

If you're playing a game, on the other hand, then the goal is to keep playing.

Work is a grind. It is compelled labor. It is heartless and soulless and designed to please another and generate capital, which is used to make more work and generate more capital. We give ourselves permission to opt out when we do work, to depersonalize it and dehumanize it and forgive our ethical shortcuts.

Games, on the other hand, are voluntary. Games have rules that we choose, and we choose to play games that reflect who we are. When we play a game, we can go all in, because it's personal. Not necessarily the winning or the losing, but the playing. The way we play is part of who we see ourselves becoming.

When we see the "work" we do as part of a game, with moves instead of failures, with outcomes instead of tragedies, we're more likely to bring the right spirit to our work. Whatever happens is part of the game—that's why we're playing it.

But not all games are the same.

James Carse wrote about the idea of finite and infinite games. A finite game is one with a winner and a loser. A finite game has rules, yes, but it also has an end. The goal of a finite game, then, is to win, to be the last man standing.

The industrial age embraced the idea of finite games. Market share is a finite game. Hiring someone from a competitor is a finite game as well—you have this all-star; your competitor does not. Every season of the NFL is a finite game, with just one team winning and everyone else walking away a loser.

Infinite games, on the other hand, are played for the privilege of playing. *The purpose of an infinite game is to allow the other players to play better.* The goal of your next move is to encourage your fellow game players to make their next moves even better.

As you've guessed, the connection economy thrives on the infinite game (and vice versa). Because connections aren't a zero-sum investment, because ideas that spread benefit all they touch, there isn't an overwhelming need for a winner (and many losers).

In the finite game, there's pressure to be the one, the one in a million. The problem with one in a million is that with those odds, there are seven thousand other people on the planet who are as good as (or better than) you are. Winning a finite game in a connected world is a sucker's bet.

In any finite game with high stakes, it's obvious that it will quickly become work, that you'll be under pressure to take steroids, cut corners, and abandon generosity in favor of focusing on the end.

Our best art is strenuous. But it's not strenuous in service of creating scarcity and of winning a finite game. It's strenuous because it's personal and generous.

Infinite games bring abundance and they bring the satisfaction of creating art that matters.

Play.

The Game Doesn't End Until It's Over

At the dawn of the Internet age, I took what felt like a huge risk. I bootstrapped an online-marketing company (we invented ethical online direct mail) and grew it, thanks to some outside funding, to about seventy employees.

We were big, we were doing significant projects for good clients, and we were barely breaking even (in a good month). Our investment money was running out, and if we didn't make some sales soon, we were going to have to either go beg for more money or fold—and a lot of good people would lose their jobs.

This was our moment of maximum risk. As founder, inventor, and rainmaker, I felt a huge burden. I needed to make sales, and now.

At a sales call in New York with a famous brand, the usual was happening. The account execs and marketing guys, having nothing better to do, were beating my colleague and me up. They were criticizing our work, talking about how expensive we were, and riffing about how smart the competition appeared to be.

In that moment, the reality of the infinite game came to me. If saving this company meant doing this every single day, I didn't want to do it. If I was so desperate to make each and every sale, then those sales would not reflect what we were able to do; they would merely be what the client was willing to buy that day. This wasn't art; it was a perversion of it.

While it would have been tragic and painful to have this business fail, I decided in that moment that it was better to fail than it was to lead my team down a path of mediocrity and abuse.

Ten minutes into the hourlong meeting, I turned to the people we were pitching, closed my laptop, and said, "You know, it seems as though we're not the right company for you. We do what we do, and we're proud of how we do it. If this isn't for you, I'm sorry to have wasted your time." And then I got up to leave. My stunned colleague stood up and started to follow.

You can probably guess what happened. The minute it was clear that we weren't desperate, the moment we started to lead instead of beg, the sale was made. We made more sales in the eight weeks that followed than we had in the two years before.

The game is infinite if you play it that way. You get to keep making your art as long as you are willing to make the choices that let you make your art.

Infinite Games, Art, and Generosity

Once you see the truth of the infinite game, Lewis Hyde's connection between art and generosity makes even more sense.

For something to be art, there has to be a gift. The gift creates connection and a bond, and those connections lie at the heart of the connection economy. Connections lead to more value, and thus the game continues.

A transaction, even steven, pushes people apart. A gift creates an imbalance; it strengthens the tribe; it moves the game forward.

Scarcity and market share and monopolies and profit maximization seek to suck energy from the system. Industrialists want the system to calm down, to become organized and productive and, most of all, profitable. Artists want to *add* energy to the system, to shake it up, to keep the game moving forward.

Artists don't give gifts as an alternative to doing a favor. They're not trying to incur a commercial debt; they're not networking their way to the top. Artists are playing the infinite game, and every gift they contribute allows them to keep playing the game.

Just Like No One Else

Artists Are Restless

We can't wait to play again.

Art is a process, not an object, and it's a process that never ends. Games that are infinite invite us to continue playing, to advance the ball, to set it up for the next person. How can you not want to keep playing that game?

Neophilia

Awesomeness has a half-life. You grow accustomed to every new marvel and miracle. You forget that a visit to a great library was once precious and astounding. You forget that you didn't see color TV until you were fifteen or a cellphone until you were forty, that the murder rate in New York City was four times as high when you arrived than when you moved away. And you forget that it was once cool to say "cool" and wear blue jeans, that "under God" wasn't always part of the Pledge of Allegiance.

We forget.

—Kurt Andersen, *True Believers*

And we're forgetting faster and more often than ever before. We're in love with the new, and it seems as though there will never be enough newness and that it will never arrive fast enough. We've built a postdeception society, one where our future is created by those who replace the status quo, not those who defend it.

Galumphing (and *Funktionslust*)

Galumphing is the seemingly useless elaboration and orna-
mentation of activity. It is profligate, excessive, exaggerated,
uneconomical. We galumph when we hop instead of walk,
when we take the scenic route instead of the efficient one,
when we play a game whose rules demand a limitation of our
powers, when we are interested in means rather than in ends.

—Stephen Nachmanovitch

My new favorite word in German is *funktionslust*. It describes the
love of doing something merely for the sake of doing it, not simply
because it's likely to work. It's the player who wants to come in off
the bench even though it's too late to win the game and the chef
who puts extra care into an omelet that someone ordered for seven
dollars from the late-night hotel menu.

Not because it's his job but because he can.

Artists play. We don't analyze our return on investment or seek
shortcuts. We are playing, not working, and the long way is often
the best way to get to where we're going, because sometimes we're
not going anywhere.

When we intentionally galumph, we're using our bodies to cue
our minds that it's time for *funktionslust*. We're setting ourselves
to put our souls into the work, because otherwise, why do it at all?

If you play in a league where you're not allowed to change the
rules, it's entirely possible that obedience and rigorous training are
your best options. For the rest of us, there's an understanding that
the rules keep changing, and we might as well enjoy the process of
changing them.

Taught in Art School

Rarely is the discussion about how to hold the brush or how to mix the paints. Art school is about rejection, vision, and commitment. Art school teaches both a vocabulary that allows you to talk intelligently about your art and the demand that you use that vocabulary to make better art.

When a nonartist reads about the typical art-school assignment, it sounds alien, dangerous, and dramatically unappealing because it is so antiindustrial, so fraught with personal risk and so likely to end up in crying. The safety zone for an artist is different from the comfort zone most of the world lives in, and it can take months or years to unbrainwash the art student so she can embrace these interactions instead of fleeing from them.

The art teacher will assign visual puzzles, dead ends disguised as useful exercises, as well as the creation of deeply personal narratives. The assignment doesn't seem to have anything much to do with putting pencil to paper, yet on inspection it turns out to have *everything* to do with it.

Technique is second (or even sixth). Commitment and play come first. The ability to question authority and the status quo. An openness to the blank slate . . .

When the result isn't the only point, then of course you're going to spend more effort on process and intent.

This might end up in crying.

If you're not prepared to cry about it, I'm not sure you're making art.

And if you're not prepared to dance in anticipation, you're definitely not making art.

How Long Should Art Take?

It might take seven years for a fast-moving Internet company to become an overnight success. It took the gay-rights movement a generation to legalize marriage in even one state. A teacher might need fourteen classes before she starts making an impact on her students. A blog doesn't hit its stride for a year or more.

Art almost never works as fast as you want it to, and the more you need it to work, the slower it happens.

The Rough Edges

In the name of productivity and mass-market acceptance, the industrialist sands off the rough edges.

The artist understands that the rough edges are the entire point.

"I Don't Have Anything to Say"

Of course you don't.

And Bob Marley didn't know how to play "Get Up, Stand Up" when he started, and Jane Austen wasn't a particularly good writer on the first day, and Valerie Jarrett knew nothing about domestic policy at first, either.

The cost of speaking up isn't what it used to be. The cost of raising your hand, making a connection, or putting your idea into the world is vanishingly small. And because the cost is so low, the risk is small as well.

> We know things could work better and that takes questioning what is, imagining what could be, and then trying to do something about it. Regardless of whether you work on Wall Street, at a nonprofit fighting hunger, or in city government, I urge you to reject complacency.
>
> —Jacqueline Novogratz, founder of Acumen Fund

You don't make art after you become an artist. You become an artist by ceaselessly making art.

What Every Artist Needs

If you're related to or married to or work for or have an artist work for you (or if you're an artist and want to share this with your team), here are a few tactical thoughts on happiness and productivity.

Don't question the commitment to the mission. It's not helpful to kindly suggest that the artist might want to think about taking a day job to tide things over or giving up or settling down or lowering the bar. The artist thinks about these things every single day, and she doesn't need you to remind her that it's possible to trade in her life and her dream for a better job so she can buy more industrialized luxuries and trinkets.

After the work is done, don't question the tactics, especially if you haven't been asked. The time to brainstorm about the very best way to interact with the market is while the art is being created, not after it has failed.

On the other hand, it's totally appropriate to ask your artist if she wants to discuss how to improve the chances that her audience will understand her art better.

Reassurance is futile. You will never be able to contribute enough reassurance to bridge the artist over the ongoing chasm that every decision and every project and every tactic brings with it. Artists need significant reassurance that they have chosen a worthy path and that you have their back. But reassurance about the work itself must come from within.

The best question you can ask an artist is "How is this going to work?"

Try to differentiate between the critical input of what one person (you) thinks about the art and the difficult empathetic understanding of what someone who isn't you thought about the art. You might not like it, but it's not fair to universalize and say that *no one* is going to like it. If you're not able to understand the work from the audience's point of view, probably better to say nothing.

The artist needs your unwavering commitment to her mission. This is the largest price you pay for being with and supporting an artist, and yes, you can probably invest even more time, passion, and money into doing this than you already do.

Part of supporting the mission is pushing the artist to be *more* committed, not less, pushing for more focus and edge and weirdness, not less. Eddie Murphy doesn't need people telling him to make yet another dumb movie for a lot of money—he needs support so he'll get back on track and make a great movie, for free if he has to.

The artist doesn't need to be given an out to avoid making art. The artist doesn't need reminders about reality or lawyers or regulations or even the rules of physics. The artist merely needs to be encouraged and cajoled and supported to make better art.

It Will All Be Okay, Because It's Always Okay

Someone asked me what advice I would give to my twenty-two-year-old MBA self. Most people, apparently, tell their earlier selves to buy Google stock, marry the rejected boyfriend, or move to a certain town—things they could do that would change the course of their life if they had to do it over.

I wouldn't change a thing, even the epic professional disasters, because every one of them is responsible for what I get to do now, and I can't imagine a better gig. But the one thing I wish I had known then was that whatever happens, things are going to be fine in the end, that the pain is part of the journey, and that without the pain there really isn't a journey worth going on.

It's not all okay because everything works. As we all know, everything *doesn't* work.

No, it doesn't all work, but you always get to dance. Win or lose, you get to play. I would tell myself not to put so much emotional baggage on every project and every interaction. The goal is to keep playing, not to win.

Reassurance doesn't scale, and being told that every project is going to work isn't helpful. What is useful is knowing that the journey is the point, and that the day my laptop started on fire in the middle of a sales call, the time I was threatened with arrest by a vice president at AOL, the nearly missed payrolls and the empty stares— all of those things are part of the art.

At the end of a project, the end of the day, and the end of the game, you can look yourself in the mirror and remind yourself that at least you got to dance.

The Highs Aren't as High

One of the things the professional artist gives up is the thrill of the manic high. I used to be manic, about twenty years ago, when there was a sliver of something working. Things were really brutal at work, with rejections and near-business-death experiences coming daily, and I grabbed hold of any positive feedback really tightly.

Now, I'm delighted to say, not so much. Which means the highs aren't as high. The successes are about the privilege of doing more work, not about winning. When my Kickstarter project for this book met its funding goal in less than three hours, I didn't do the line-kicking dance reserved for TV celebrations. Instead, I took out my laptop and got to work. That is the greatest privilege I can imagine.

Never a Better Time

Sometimes you get lucky and find yourself in the right place at just the right time. If that happens and you don't realize it, though, you will probably waste the opportunity.

I think that's where we are right now. The right place. The right time. And you might not realize it.

This is a lousy time to be an industrialist, a lousy time to hope for reliable, predictable demand. A lousy time to expect to extract unreasonable profits by making average stuff for average people. A lousy time, especially, to be a well-paid middle manager who does what he's told in exchange for a safe job.

On the other hand, there's never been a better time to have something to say, to embrace change, and to see the world differently. There's never been a better time to make connections instead of stuff. And most of all, there's never been a better time to make art.

Who Wants to Be a Millionaire?

Most of the time, that's how we encourage art. Who wants to be famous? Who wants to be on TV? Who wants a standing ovation or kudos at the meeting or a promotion?

I think there's a better question:

Do you care enough to fail?

Your Biggest Failure

Amazingly, it's not that great thing you did with good intent that ended in disaster.

No, your biggest failure is the thing you dreamed of contributing but didn't find the guts to do. This is the something that those in power want you to overlook, because it undermines their attempts to keep you in line.

The biggest black mark on your working résumé is the road not taken, the project not initiated, and the art not made.

Don't Buy Their Cynicism

An insecure consumer is a good consumer, and an unsure employee is a compliant one as well. The insecure consumer is easily swayed by promises and will eagerly sign up for anything that promises security. The unsure employee is putty in the hands of the manager seeking to give directions.

When you decide you're not talented enough or not ready to speak up, when you buy the line about not being well trained or well born enough to make a difference, you cede your power to those in authority.

The cynic who doesn't vote because it won't change anything has guaranteed that nothing will change. The musician who waits for a record label to call (while hating the labels for their greed and arrogance) has handed over all her power to the labels.

The cost of being wrong is dwarfed by the cost of not trying.

I Did It, I Made It, I Said It

It is so much easier to fail than it used to be.

So much easier to put something into the world and see it not work.

You don't need a building or a degree or an ad budget. You don't need anyone's permission.

What an opportunity. Please don't let a hundred years of brainwashing cause you to waste it.

You learn to swim by swimming.
You learn courage by couraging.

—Mary Daly, as quoted by Brené Brown

Start Your Journey Before You See the End

The resistance wants to be reassured. It wants a testable plan. It wants to know that before it endures the pain, it is guaranteed the prize at the end.

"Give me more case studies, more examples, more reassurance. Give me proof!"

The lizard brain has succeeded in making you stuck. The best art is made by artists who don't know how it's going to work out in the end. The rest of the world is stuck with the brainwashed culture that the industrialists gave us, the culture of fear and compliance.

But culture is a choice. You don't have to accept a culture of fear or a culture of failure. Right now, just down the hall or just up the street, is another artist, someone filled with hope and excitement, someone choosing a different culture, even though he's in the same town, the same industry, and the same economy you are.

Others have always done that art, always chosen that culture of hope, but you haven't done it enough ("too risky," the lizard says), because you've been held back by a need for proof, by a reliance on assurance, and by the fear of humiliation.

Art is a project; it is not a place. You will build your dream house and it will burn down. You will start your business and it will succeed, until it doesn't, and then you'll move on. You will stand on-stage and speak from the heart, and some people in the audience (perhaps just one person in the audience) won't get you, won't accept you, won't embrace you.

That's what art is.

Art is a leap into the void, a chance to give birth to your genius and to make magic where there was no magic before.

You are capable of this. You've done it before and you're going to do it again. The very fact that it might not work is precisely why you should and must do this. What a gift that there isn't a sure thing, a guarantee, and a net.

It's entirely possible that there won't be a standing ovation at the end of your journey.

That's okay.

At least you lived.

Don't Waste This Platform

As I'm writing this, I'm drinking tea (made with leaves shipped through a supply chain more than three thousand miles long) out of a glass bottle (smelted at a temperature unobtainable by humans not long ago), and I'm working on a computer that would have cost a million dollars ten years ago, except you couldn't buy one at any price, and the computer is connected to the Internet via Wi-Fi (it's all a miracle).

We're living in a moment of time, the first moment of time, when a billion people are connected, when your work is judged (more than ever before) based on what you do rather than who you are, and when credentials, access to capital, and raw power have been dwarfed by the simple question "Do I care about what you do?"

We built this world for you. Not so you would watch more online videos, keep up on your feeds, and LOL with your high school friends. We built it so you could do what you're capable of. Without apology and without excuse.

Go.

yes I said yes I will Yes

—Molly Bloom in James Joyce's *Ulysses*

APPENDIX ONE

True-Life Stories of Fourteen Real Artists

"Look Like Jill"

Jill Greenberg took my picture when we were both teenagers. Sometime after that, she became one of the most important fine-art photographers in the world.

We live in a society where just about everyone has a camera. And when everyone has a camera, just about everyone will take pictures. In that sort of marketplace, with that sort of competition, how is it possible to accomplish anything?

It's easy to describe but difficult to do: Jill relentlessly chose her own path. She began by embracing Photoshop, a tool that was shunned by all but a few photographers, who believed that all the work had to happen before the shot was taken, not after.

Then she sought out difficult topics. She took pictures of zombielike presidential candidates, angry bears, and crying babies. And she did it without reserve. A quick look at Jill's portfolio shows that she consistently refuses to hold back. The pictures are all presented at the volume of eleven.

Most of all, Jill's pictures look like Jill's pictures. No one hires her to take pictures that look like they were taken by someone else or that look like they were taken by *anyone* else. In fact, art directors on a budget often hire other photographers with the instruction to "look like Jill."

Most of the people with a camera don't have the guts to make the decisions that Jill did, and to stick it out for as long as Jill did, and to take as many pictures for no pay as Jill did. Jill sees what the rest of us don't, she makes art in a way that's unique, and she has the guts to show us what she's made.

The Lipstick Chick

As the first VP of special projects and new media at Estée Lauder, Angela Kapp brought this cosmetics giant into the digital age.

She did it when no one had a clue about how to do that. There was no manual. She couldn't look at L'Oréal or Revlon and copy them, because they were totally clueless and afraid. Angela was clueless (like the rest of us) but bold.

And so she tried things. She broke things. She spoke up and she spoke out. She didn't code, but she figured out how to find and cajole and encourage people who did. She went to conferences and shared what she'd learned and learned from others who were there to share. And then she repeated the process.

Angela understood that her best asset wasn't the secrets of what she'd learned; it was the guts to do the next thing. So she paid her secrets forward, put them into the infinite game of learning, and learned more in exchange.

Ten years after she began, she exited the Estée Lauder Companies at the top of her game to make a ruckus in other countries with other clients. Years later, the people at Estée Lauder still miss Angela, and the people she taught are still following the path she set.

Abandoning Competence

Charlie Osmond is already a star. *Esquire UK* picked him as entrepreneur of the year, and he has started several profitable companies that employ hundreds of people.

He knows how to start and to run service-oriented consulting practices. He's also aware of his weaknesses, so he has spent a ton of time and energy addressing, for example, his ability to manage, in order to become a well-rounded company founder and manager. This is smart industrialist thinking, and it pays off.

And he's had enough of this.

Starting in 2013, Charlie Osmond is doubling down on his strengths and pursuing his dream instead of maintaining his (successful) status quo. He's risking his reputation and his momentum by starting a new company, Triptease, that won't be a consultancy, won't be focused on business customers, and may very well redefine what we see when we share travel ideas online. And it might just fail.

When he talks about the new venture, you can see the thing that Charlie has that's rare. The combination of confidence and fear, the artist's ability to see what's out there and imagine what the next thing might be. But most of all, the willingness to disappoint (if it doesn't work) and to walk into a new place where he is quite likely to be momentarily incompetent.

The Patron Saint of Kickstarter

Amanda Palmer is the Internet's rock star. Since leaving the Dresden Dolls in 2008, Amanda has persistently and single-mindedly defined how the independent musician can make a living and make a ruckus.

Her most recent overnight success was her record-breaking Kickstarter campaign in mid-2012. Of course, it wasn't an overnight success at all; it was the work of years of dues paying, art making, and planning. Yes, she raised more than a million dollars in thirty days . . . with no label, no A&R team, no venture capitalists, and no paid media. But it took her years to build the tribe that would support her through the process and spread the word about her audacious plans.

If you had asked Amanda whether she was doing all those free gigs and free tracks and free events so that a year later she could have a successful Kickstarter campaign, I have no doubt that the second word of her half-unprintable response would have been "no." If you asked her if she spends so much time with her fans online and off just so she can make a living later, the answer would be obvious. She does it because giving her work to her fans is the privilege of her life.

"Get Your Face Out of Facebook"

At first glance, John Sherigan appears to be in the waste business. His company processes millions of pounds of e-waste every month, breaking it down, recycling it, and minimizing the impact on landfills. Your iPad probably contains some of his aluminum. "It's a simple business; we take in electronics and turn them into plastics, glass and metals." The industrialist sees this as a factory-focused process. Figure out how to do the processing for less, hire cheap, enforce your systems, and repeat.

John, on the other hand, sees his business as part of a bigger ecosystem. He and his team aren't selling 'a commodity process. Instead, they spend their lives on the road, making human connections, one person at a time, face to face, earning the privilege of being trusted. They spend their time solving new problems, sharing big ideas, understanding what's important.

When it's time to raise money or open a new location or find a new partner, John understands that merely presenting a spreadsheet of assets and liabilities isn't the way to move forward. There are plenty of alternatives if you're the maker of a commodity.

What's scarce is trust.

What Is He, Crazy?

Willie Jackson quit his job, a high-paying, fast-track job with a consulting firm. He did it right after he bought a house, and with no plan in mind.

Why does a twentysomething with a mortgage do something as crazy as that?

Because it wasn't crazy at all. It was life.

Willie Jackson understood that he'd ended up working to live and decided he'd enjoy the next hundred years of life on earth a lot more if he started living to work instead. Since that day a year or so ago, he's moved to a new city, made dozens of new friends, built a network of trusted colleagues, signed on plenty of new clients, done an enormous amount of work with people he believed in, and danced on the edge the entire time.

Has he done something to make him famous? Not yet. That's not the point. The point is that he walked away from the obvious system to build a nonobvious life.

The Thirty-six-Billion-Dollar Art Project

Cynthia Carroll was recently made CEO of Anglo American, a multibillion-dollar mining company. It's responsible for finding most of the diamonds, platinum, and other essential mined metals in the world. She was its first woman CEO, the first without a long history in mining, and the first who wasn't from South Africa. The stakes couldn't be higher: This hundred-year-old company employs nearly 150,000 people worldwide.

Given the conservative nature of the company, it's shocking to note that the first significant act of her tenure was to fly to the notorious Rustenburg mine and go deep inside the "dark, hot, wet and steep" workplace, hundreds of feet underground, a place where, on average, forty people a year die in workplace accidents.

Stunned by the enormity of what she saw, Carroll did something no mining CEO in a similar situation had ever done before. *She voluntarily shut down the mine.* Not in reaction to an uproar (there wasn't one). Not as a PR stunt (two days shut down and then back to normal). No, she shut down the largest and most profitable platinum mine in the world for nine weeks merely because she couldn't abide the danger. She created such an uproar that the CEO of the division quit.

Carroll went even further. She organized a productive working relationship among the unions, the government, and the mining companies and engaged in a multiyear battle to redefine what got measured and how mining was done. The next year, as a direct result of one person's art project, fatalities at this mine dropped by half, and they continue to fall.

How do we know this story? Because Cynthia Carroll told us. She aired Anglo's laundry, shared the stats, explained the realities of what her options were, and opened herself up to being criticized, ostracized, and unloved.

No rule book, no paintbrush. This was high-stakes art, the willingness to work without a map and to forge new relationships.

Salmon Don't Vote

In the words of former secretary of the interior Bruce Babbitt, "cabinet secretaries who stir up too much controversy can and do lose their jobs." That's exactly what he risked when he proposed to tear down the Elwha River dam, a hundred-year-old public-works project that was both obsolete and decimating the salmon population.

Expecting nothing but applause, Babbitt held a press conference to announce his big idea. He was immediately condemned by senators, newspapers, and even his boss.

Art projects are rarely met with unanimous approval. If they were obvious, everyone would do one.

So he got to work. His team did cost estimates, hydrologic computations, sediment studies, and more. And none of it changed anyone's mind. The country has more than seventy-five thousand dams, and not one had been torn down the way Babbitt was proposing. Data weren't going to make a difference. Like most places where art works, this was an emotional decision, not a mathematical one.

A few years later, the persistent secretary presided over the demolition of a much smaller, even more obsolete dam in North

Carolina. With less fanfare and thus less opposition, Babbitt was able to tear it down. In less than a year, the fish population, gone for forty years, returned. Now he didn't have just statistics—he had living, breathing, emotional proof that demolishing a dam was a worthwhile effort.

The story was the output of his work. A story that resonated with people.

In 2012 the Elwha dam came down.

Turning Aquaculture Upside Down

When San Persand was twenty-one years old, he was working at an aquaculture facility, helping to grow fish. The fish were housed in large cube-shaped pens, with each side covered in fish netting. This design permitted the cube to be hauled out of the water and the grown fish to be harvested.

The problem was that the sides of the netting would become encrusted with seaweed, and no fresh water could flow through, so the fish would suffocate and die. The seaweed threatened to destroy the economics of this fish farm (and many others).

Persand, with no authority, no engineering training, and no instruction manual, invented a solution—another art project. He suggested replacing the square tanks with cylindrical ones. Everything was the same, except the tubes were easy to rotate. Every time the seaweed grew on the bottom of the cylinder, the farm would rotate the cylinder, exposing the seaweed on the bottom to the sun and air above the surface, killing it without affecting the fish within.

Art is where you find it.

Strategy Is Second

Like many entrepreneurs and consultants, Anne McCrossan understands the mechanics that are driving social media to change things. That's not scarce. But that understanding of the nuts and bolts isn't why people hire her firm, Visceral Business, or choose to work with her in her network.

Being smart is second.

No, the attractor is a willingness to put things on the line, to work all the way to the edge of impossible. No strategy memo can bring that humanity to the table; only the artist's insistence on caring can do it. She says, "We can develop business cultures in a different way, a way in which people can and want to be part of it, respond and make a difference." That kind of statement gets you thrown out of a lot of pitches, causes rolled eyes, and is a tough sell. Until it's not a tough sell. Until you find the audience for this kind of art.

Organizations and coworkers notice when a single individual pours herself into something without much thought about the downside. Taking action when you're scared—you can't look down, just straight ahead. Taking action sometimes just for the love of it. It becomes an almost alchemical process, transforming a valid strategy into something that actually connects.

Building a Movement Out of Town

Hugh Weber understands that not all big ideas, not all important art, and not all movements start in big cities. He's the founder of OTA, a creative collective based in South Dakota that is nothing less than a catalyst for a regionwide explosion in creativity and possibility.

When he started, he thought that he'd have to single-handedly build this movement himself. What he discovered, though, was, "I've been forced to recognize that I'm not in this alone and that I can't do it alone. The people who have stepped forward to support, engage and help lead this effort have humbled me and transformed my perspective on community."

The hard work, it turns out, isn't in booking gigs or being brilliant. The hard work is in persuading others to see the same vision, to use the same can-do attitude that grew up on the farm and apply it to building an eclectic, creative community. "I think the primary difference is simply a perspective of possibility. Our region is remarkably well suited for problem solving. When there's a flood, blizzard or fire, everyone comes together, works together and survives together. But when we think about something bigger, innovative or possibility focused, we seem to believe that has to happen alone in our basement."

The connection economy amplifies the makers of change. There are people in the community, even in the flyover towns that New Yorkers sneer at, who are just waiting to be asked, just waiting to exercise their ability to be weird. The job of the community organizer is simple: not to find the right answer but to find the right audience, the right segment of the community. Connect them, amplify the positive outliers, and repeat until change happens.

How Much Is Enough?

Ben Cohen is the tenth-highest-scoring rugby player in the history of the United Kingdom. At the age of thirty-three, near the peak of his game, he was offered a lucrative three-year contract and he turned it down.

Cohen decided to use his fame and his resources to work full time with a foundation he founded to stop bullying and homophobia.

Why would an athlete in a sport where the earning window is already limited walk away from a three-year contract? Why would a married, straight man decide to devote years of his life to fighting homophobia?

That's part of the hard work of art. Art can never be about maximizing short-term profit, because the dictates of short-term profit almost always point to shortcuts and the rigorous work of optimizing productivity. The hard work that Ben Cohen is doing involves a longer arc and the chance to pay attention not to his wallet but to what matters to him.

For a season or two, Ben Cohen is going to be missed by his teammates. But his choice to do this art project gives him the chance to leave a legacy and to do work that would be missed if he were gone.

That's Beautiful

Joey Roth picked himself. He picked himself to bring his wooden compass to the world. And his stunning ceramic stereo speakers. And his handmade, self-watering plant pots. He sells them on his Web site and he has no shortage of customers. The world beats a path to his door.

Not the whole world, of course. Just a tiny slice of the world. Most people in the world don't brew loose-leaf tea, so they're not interested in his groundbreaking glass pot. And even people who do brew tea (most of them, anyway) don't care about his sort of beauty or don't know what he made.

But that's okay, because there are still plenty of people who *do* know and *do* care. There are still plenty of people who have spread the word, who have bought one of his remarkable objects as a gift or for themselves.

In any other universe, a craftsperson like Joey Roth would be disrespected by the milling passersby at a craft show somewhere. They'd be measuring him against the work they're used to, not seeking something new and vibrant. Instead, by picking himself and (most of all) by making work that resonates, he brings his art to people who care about it, daily.

Picked

Jenny Rosenstrach had one of those fancy New York City media jobs that you see in the movies. And then she didn't.

Jenny wanted to be a writer. Well, she already was a writer, and a good one. What she wasn't was published. Her work needed an audience.

For ten years Jenny regularly kept a diary of every meal she prepared with her husband and then, after they came on the scene, with her two children as well. Like Steve Martin, she was focused on precision, on understanding, on discovering the art in the journey she was on. She had already committed to something.

It was time for a book deal. But instead of spending two years trying and then waiting to get picked, Jenny started a blog (it's called *Dinner: A Love Story*). No connections, no fancy technology, no expensive investments, just Jenny and her writing.

Day by day, week by week, the blog attracted an audience. The audience members connected—with Jenny and with one another. They had something in common, and Jenny spoke to them in a way that gave their dreams a voice.

Right on schedule, two years later, a publisher eagerly published her book, and it became the best-selling cookbook in America within three days of publication.

Jenny gave her art a place to grow by picking herself.

I knew I had been transformed, moved by the revelation that human beings create art, that to be an artist was to see what others could not.

I had no proof that I had the stuff to be an artist, though I hungered to be one. . . . I wondered if I had really been called as an artist. I didn't mind the misery of a vocation but I dreaded not being called.

—Patti Smith, *Just Kids*

APPENDIX TWO

V Is for Vulnerable:
An Artist's Abecedary

ANXIETY is experiencing failure in advance. Tell yourself enough vivid stories about the worst possible outcome of your work and you'll soon come to believe them. Worry is not preparation, and anxiety doesn't make you better.

BIRL that log. Find your balance by losing it, and commit to keeping your feet in motion until you're birling and the log is spinning. The log isn't going to spin itself, you know. A spinning log is stable for a while, but not forever. That's why birling is worth watching.

COMMITMENT is the only thing that gets you through the chasm. Commitment takes you from "That's a fine idea" to "It's done." Commitment is risky, because if you fail, it's on you. But without commitment, you will fail, because art unshipped isn't art.

DANCE with fear. Dance with done. Dance with the resistance. Dance with each other. Dance with art.

EFFORT isn't the point, impact is. If you solve the problem in three seconds but have the guts to share it with me, it's still art. And if you move ten thousand pounds of granite but the result doesn't connect with me, I'm sorry for your calluses, but you haven't made art, at least not art for me.

FEEDBACK is either a crutch or a weapon. Use feedback to make your work smaller, safer, and more likely to please everyone (and fail in the long run). Or use it as a lever, to further push yourself to embrace what you fear (and what you're capable of).

GIFTS are the essence of art. Art isn't made as part of an even exchange, it is your chance to create imbalance, which leads to connection. To share your art is a requirement of making it.

HEROES are people who take risks for the right reasons. Real art is a heroic act. Hipsters, on the other hand, are pretenders who haven't risked a thing but like to play the part.

INITIATIVE is the privilege of picking yourself. You're not given initiative, you take it. Pick yourself. If you're still not getting what you want, it may be because you're not making good enough art, often enough.

JOY is different from pleasure or delight or fun. Joy is the satisfaction of connection, the well-earned emotion you deserve after shipping art that made a difference.

A **K**NIFE works best when it has an edge. To take the edge off, to back off, to play it safe, to smooth it out, to please the uninterested masses—that's not what the knife is for.

L is for **LMNO**, which used to be a single letter of the alphabet. The artist seeks to break apart the unbreakable and to combine the uncombinable. And L is for lonely, because everyone is, and the artist does the endless work of helping us conquer that loneliness.

MORE is not the goal of the artist. Better is the artist's dream. Better connection is the point of the work. More stuff leads to a world of scarcity, while better connected creates abundance.

"NO" feels safe, while "yes" is dangerous indeed. Yes to possibility and yes to risk and yes to looking someone in the eye and telling her the truth.

ONE-BUTTOCK playing is what Ben Zander would have you do. To play the piano and mean it. To sit up, to lean in, to perform as if this were your very best, your very last chance to let the song inside of you get out.

PAIN is the truth of art. Art is not a hobby or a pastime. It is the result of an internal battle royal, one between the quest for safety and the desire to matter.

QUALITY, like feedback, is a trap. To focus on reliably meeting specifications (a fine definition of quality) is to surrender the real work, which is to matter. Quality of performance is a given; it's not the point.

REMIX, reuse, respect, recycle, revisit, reclaim, revere, resorb. Art doesn't repeat itself, but it rhymes.

SHAME is the flip side of vulnerability. We avoid opening ourselves to the connection art brings because we fear that we will finally be seen as the frauds we are.

TETHER is the safety cable you refuse to use. Art feels fatal, because art makes us vulnerable. The Flying Wallendas, the legendary trapeze-swinging and tightrope-walking family, have a slogan: "If we fall, we die."

UMBRELLAS keep you from getting wet. Why on earth would you use one? Getting wet is the entire point.

VULNERABLE is the only way we can feel when we truly share the art we've made. When we share it, when we connect, we have shifted the power and made ourselves naked in front of the person we've given the gift of our art to. We have no excuses, no manual to point to, no standard operating procedures to protect us. And that is part of our gift.

The **W**ARRANTY of merchantability is a legal principle that guarantees that something you buy will do what the seller promises it will. Your work in art doesn't come with one. Your art might not work and your career might not work, either. If it doesn't work today, it might not work tomorrow, either. But our practice is to persist until it does.

XEBEC is a pirate ship. The real kind, not the sort that selfish, evil, violent pretend pirates in Somalia use. Artist pirates steal in order to remix and then give back.

YOUTH isn't a number; it's an attitude. So many disruptive artists, even the old ones, have been youngsters. Art isn't a genetic or chronological destiny; it's a choice, open to anyone willing to trade pain in exchange for magic.

ZABAGLIONE is a delightful Italian dessert consisting mostly of well-whipped foam. It takes a lot of effort to make by hand. Each batch comes out a little different from the previous one. It's often delicious. It doesn't last long. It's evanescent. And then you have to (get to) make another batch.

ACKNOWLEDGMENTS

Robert Irwin, Joseph Campbell, Lewis Hyde, Patti Smith, Steve Martin, Brené Brown, Ben Zander, James Elkins, Tina Eisenberg, George Lakoff, James Joyce, Robert Pirsig, Jeffrey Fry, Oscar Wilde, Teri Tobias, Neil Gaiman, A. F. Palmer, Elizabeth Gilbert, Lisa DiMona, Ishita Gupta, Lisa Gansky, Susan Cain, Jacqueline Novogratz, Sasha Dichter, Xeni Jardin, Mark Fraunfelder, Cory Doctorow, Steve Dennis, Jonathan Sackner Bernstein, Carla Lisio, James Carse, Nancy Hathaway, Pema Chödron, Susan Piver, Bernadette Jiwa, Michelle Welsch, Jim Leff.

And Adrian Zackheim, Niki Papadopoulos, Will Weisser, Natalie Horbachevsky, Joseph Perez, and Catherine E. Oliver.

Of course, Helene, Alex, and Mo.

A serious *thank you* to my blog readers, for giving me their attention and letting me try out many of these ideas for the first time there. You might even find a classic post or two in this book. You can read my blog every day for free by Googling *Seth's blog*.

For an annotated bibliography, visit theicarusdeception.com.